Say My Name

The Third Commandment:
It's Probably Not What You Think!

Dr. Melvin G. Barney, Esq.

Trilogy Christian Publishers
A Wholly Owned Subsidiary of Trinity Broadcasting Network
2442 Michelle Drive
Tustin, CA 92780

Cover design by: Scott A. Perry, artist for hire, www.artforhire.com.

For information, address Trilogy Christian Publishing
Rights Department, 2442 Michelle Drive, Tustin, Ca 92780.
Trilogy Christian Publishing/ TBN and colophon are trademarks of Trinity Broadcasting Network.

For information about special discounts for bulk purchases, please contact Trilogy Christian Publishing.

Manufactured in the United States of America

Trilogy Disclaimer: The views and content expressed in this book are those of the author and may not necessarily reflect the views and doctrine of Trilogy Christian Publishing or the Trinity Broadcasting Network.

10 9 8 7 6 5 4 3 2 1

Library of Congress Cataloging-in-Publication Data is available.

ISBN 978-1-63769-254-7 (Print Book)
ISBN 978-1-63769-255-4 (ebook)

DEDICATION

You know Who You are. And yes—I love You with all of my heart, with all of my soul, with all of my mind, and with all of my strength. This is for You.

FOREWARD

At the opening service of the 2022 Sacramento Victory Campaign, Kenneth Copeland stated the following:

> I hold in my hand a book, *Say My Name—The Third Commandment: It's Probably Not What You Think!*, Dr. Melvin G. Barney, Esq.

> And um, Dr. Melvin, where are you? I thought that was you. Stand up there, sir. I want to congratulate you! Man, this is going to be required reading for every Kenneth Copeland Bible College student. I'm not [just] reading this book, I am studying it.

> I've talked about power of attorney for years. This man is an attorney. Amen. And he knows what power of attorney is.

> Now being a graduate of [United] Theological Seminary and a Kenneth Copeland Scholar at that seminary... Thank you...

Wow. Mmmm. Mmmmm. I learn things… I thought I knew a little bit – I did know a little bit about the Name. Nobody knows at all. Yep.

Oh, *Say My Name*. Mmm mmmmm mmmmm. Oh this is good. Get the book!

I don't know how much it cost. I didn't buy it, he gave it to me. [Laughter]. They are a hundred dollars a piece, okay. [Laughter]. No.

Say My Name, Dr. Melvin G. Barney, Esq. … Amen. That thing's hot!

Now I want you to, I really want you to study this book because there's insight into that third commandment I did not know until I got this book.

Kenneth Copeland
2022 Sacramento Victory Campaign
Opening Night, May 12, 2022

Scan this QR Code to view
Kenneth Copeland's review of
Say My Name.

DR. MELVIN G. BARNEY, ESQ.

ACKNOWLEDGMENTS

Shout-out to my mother, Mrs. Eula M. Barney, who dragged me to church, taught me how to depend on God, and instilled within me a desire to live for Him.

Thanks to my near mentors, Kenneth Copeland, R. A. Vernon, Ronn Elmore, Loran Mann, and Archie Dennis (deceased), and my distant mentors, T. D. Jakes and Charles E. Blake Sr., for your teaching, modeling, wisdom, guidance, and investments in me.

To Kellie Copeland, Stephen Swisher, Dr. Jackie R. Baston, and all my United Theological Seminary instructors, mentors, and fellow Kenneth Copeland scholars: thank you for what you have invested in me.

To my church, the O Logos Alive Church family, who allowed yourselves to be my guinea pigs, as I tried out this teaching on you and watched the impact it has had on your lives.

Thank you, Andrea Adams and Brandon Barney, for your invaluable assistance with the formatting.

Iveda Williams, Sonya Jones, and Jeannine Carson for being all of my appendages. Rose Fountain, LaShonda Williams, Glenn Strother Jr., Darice Murray, Sylvia Jackson, Dorothy Horne, Taylor Jones, Letrice Fowler, Jaqueline Joseph-Veal, Drella Hunter, Crawford Johnson, Regina Crawford, Lora Worster, Lamont and Elizabeth Benjamin, Barbara James, Jessie Patton, Kerri Banks-Henagan, Debbie Hudson, Deborah Williams, Julia Pride, Janie Taylor, Shelia Howard, Monzelle Baker, Chelsea Zimba, Toni Alston, Tracy Ward, Lori

Acknowledgements

Baldwin, JuJuan Hill, Tiffany Macon, Vera Holland, Leon and Tamiko Davis, and all of the leaders and prayer warriors of OLA Church, for making ministry easy and delightful.

To the young guys and the not-so-young women who look out for me: Julian Sutherland, Malachi Banks, Cynsere Kelly, Alex Barney, Chad Vickers, Jericho Aiello, Bridget Sutherland, and Tonette Jackson.

My fake twin sister, Aladrian Elmore, for bossing me around because she thinks she is my real sister.

Shout out to my boys, Brandon, Noah, and Alex—my greatest desire is that you can always bear witness that I practice what I preach.

My family, James and Aurelia, Richard, Aderion Sr., Marvin, and Kaye Kaye.

All of my adopted mothers. God promised me in Mark 10:29-30 that if I sold out to Him, He would give me a whole bunch of mothers. Well, He has done just that: Mother Elizabeth Slade, Mother Lois Heathman, Mother Josephine Woods, Mother Wilhelmina Williams, Mother Charlene Maxey, Mother Dorothy Miles, and Mother Mary McLennan. Also, I cannot leave out my adopted pop, Joseph Slade.

My newly discovered cousins, Tony and Mary Gordon, who are here for me in every way imaginable. You are the best things since sliced bread.

To my friends, Norman and Deborah Bolden, Byron and Michelle Samuels, Ray Washington Jr., Lynn and Erma Riley, Wayne Berry, Marvin and Annette Davis, Philip and Kathy Edwards, for inspiring me to go higher and encouraging me to do more.

Thank you, Aimee Steele, for your valuable input. You are very special.

And last but certainly not least, to my amazing, newly-wedded wife, Sherika Barney. Baby, I love you and I thank you for teaching me what real love looks like.

DR. MELVIN G. BARNEY, ESQ.

CONTENTS

PREFACE

Like many of you who will read this book, I grew up in a household in which going to church was as much a part of life as eating breakfast in the morning and doing household chores on Saturdays. It was just something that we did. Some of my earliest memories in life have me sitting in the choir stand at my mother's feet playing with my toys on the floor while she and the other ladies in the soprano section of the adult choir struggled to get their part right.

Ours was a home where we were taught what it looked like to be committed to God. When we were young, we were taken to church. When we got older, we still had to go to church. Even when we crept into those teenage, rebellious years, where we started "smelling ourselves" and thinking we were grown, there was always one area where there was no room for compromise: we had to be at church on Sunday.

I remember a Sunday when one of my brothers did not want to go, so he decided to stay in bed when he should have been getting ready. As we were walking out of the door to get into the car, before she closed the door to the house, my mother yelled upstairs to that brother, "You had better meet me at the church." He walked there that day.

I grew up in a Baptist church. When I went away for college, I eventually found myself in a Pentecostal church. After graduating from college with my MBA, I landed in a nondenominational church. For most of my life, I have had people telling me, "You are going to be a preacher." For years, my response was always, "Nope. I want to be a lawyer." Well, I am a lawyer. But I am also a preacher. And though I ran from the calling of my life for years, today, I can say I am proud to be a mouthpiece for the Lord.

When I finally made a commitment to fully walk with the Lord and let Him have His way in my life, and when I determined to saturate myself in His Word, God began to show me things about Himself. He started giving me revelations in His Word. He started exposing me to great men and women of God from whom I could absorb powerful and anointed teaching. After I sold out and stopped resisting Him, God birthed in me an intense desire for a closer relationship with Him through an intimate understanding of His Word.

This is how I landed in seminary. And that is where I was introduced to biblical Hebrew. And this is where I started clawing and clambering to go higher and dig deeper. And this was how I discovered that the third commandment, which states, "You shall not take the Name of the Lord your God in vain," does not at all mean what we have been taught it means.

Pastor Melvin G. Barney, BS, MSIA, JD, DMin

INTRODUCTION

One of the first things we teach our children, shortly after they learn to talk, is the "Now I Lay Me Down to Sleep" prayer. Every night before we tuck them in bed, we have them get on their little knees, and we watch proudly as they recite those words:

> "Now I lay me down to sleep, I pray
> the Lord my soul to keep.
> If I should die before I wake, I pray
> the Lord my soul to take."

In many a Christian household, this is their introduction to God.

At some point, we begin to take them to Sunday school or children's church. And inevitably, the day comes when, in response to our inquiry into what they learned on that day, what comes from their mouths is a summation of the Ten Commandments.

> Number 1. You shall have no other
> gods before Me.
> Number 2. You shall not create or
> worship any idol gods.

> Number 3. You shall not take the
> Name of the Lord your God in vain...
> And so on.

For some reason, the pride that welled up in us when we heard them recite the "Now I Lay Me Down to Sleep" prayer at the age of two or three revisits us when they have been introduced to the Ten Commandments. It is almost like a "rite of passage" to get there, and most of us, at some point in our past, got there.

Most of us can also attest to the fact that throughout our Christian journey, the topic of the Ten Commandments has been revisited, over and over and over again. And every time it was revisited, whether in a Sunday school class, or in the pastor's sermon, or during a Bible study, or in our own private Bible reading, all we have gotten out of the teaching on the Ten Commandments is that they are very important, and we are to take them very seriously.

Some of us have been introduced to teaching that points out the following:

- Commandments one through four are vertical commandments that tell us how to deal with God;
- Commandments six through ten are horizontal commandments that tell us how to deal with people; and
- Commandment five, the one in the middle, is a bridge commandment. It addresses how we are to treat our parents, so it has some vertical aspects to it as well as some horizontal ones.

We also, for the most part, are able to "get" the commandments. God makes it very clear that He wants first place in our lives. We get that. He is not playing when He says,

"No idols." We can understand that. The commandments that tell us how to treat each other make sense to us. We know it is wrong to murder and commit adultery and steal.

What strikes me as interesting, however, is that we also *think* we know what that third commandment means. Nevertheless, from the time the Ten Commandments were given until the present day, a great deal of confusion has surrounded this particular commandment.

"You shall not take the Name of the LORD your God in vain, for the LORD will not hold him guiltless who takes His Name in vain" (Exodus 20:7).

YHWH is the personal Name of God. God disclosed His Name, YHWH, to Moses when He commissioned him to lead the children of Israel out of Egypt.

> Then Moses said to God, "Indeed, when I come to the children of Israel and say to them, 'The God of your fathers has sent me to you,' and they say to me, 'What is His [N]ame?' what shall I say to them?" And God said to Moses, "I AM WHO I AM." And He said, "Thus you shall say to the children of Israel, 'I AM has sent me to you.'" Moreover God said to Moses, "Thus you shall say to the children of Israel: '[YHWH, Elohiym] of your fathers, the God of Abraham, the God of Isaac, and the God of Jacob, has sent me to you. *This is My [N]ame forever*, and this is My memorial to all generations.'"
>
> Exodus 3:13-15, emphasis and brackets added

Nevertheless, YHWH is the Name that the Jews would not even utter because they interpreted Exodus, chapter twenty, verse seven, very narrowly. They interpreted "You shall not take the Name of the Lord in vain…" to mean you are not even supposed to speak His Name. And in order to safeguard what they thought was this commandment, the Jews customarily left out the vowels when they wrote the Name. And whenever they spoke the Name, instead of saying YHWH, they substituted in its place the title, *Adoni*, which is Hebrew for "Lord."

That's confusion. Why would God give them His Name if He did not want them to speak it? And why would Jesus tell us to "hallow" His Name if He did not want us to know it? That defies logic. Nevertheless, that's how the Jews interpreted that commandment. Confusion.

And today, there is still confusion. In most Christian circles even now, the third commandment is generally taken to mean one or both of the following:

- We are not to profane the Name of the Lord in cursing or in hostility; and/or
- We are not to utter the Name of the Lord flippantly or disrespectfully or for the purpose of exclamation or emphasis.

While I absolutely agree that we are not to utter the Name of the Lord in cursing or in hostility, and while I absolutely agree that our practice should not be to inject things such as "G-D-it" in our conversations, I do not believe that is what this commandment is talking about.

"You shall not take the Name of the
LORD your God in vain, for the LORD

will not hold him guiltless who takes His
Name in vain" (Exodus 20:7).

Our English translations of the Scripture say, "You shall
not *take* the Name of the Lord your God in vain…" They do
not say, "You shall not *utter* the Name of the Lord your God
irreverently…"

The correct interpretation of this scripture turns on
what is meant by the words, "take…in vain." You shall not
"take" the Name of the Lord your God "in vain."

In biblical Hebrew, the word that is translated "take"
also means "carry," "lift," "bear." Further, to do something
"in vain" is to do something that is "wasteful."

Thus, when God commands us to *not* take His Name
in vain, He is expecting us to carry or tote His Name around
with us as a resource or tool to get the sought-after result, in
the same way that a carpenter carries his hammer and nails
with purpose, so he can use them to build a set of kitchen
cabinets.

The third commandment challenges us to carry God's
Name with purpose and use God's Name as a tool to cause
the will of God to be done and the promises of God to come
to pass. To have access to the Name of the Lord but not use
it to change the things that are out of alignment with His
promises is like carrying an umbrella around with you but
not using it when it starts to rain. That's a waste. That's toting the umbrella in vain.

When we are not using the Lord's Name to accomplish
what He promises us in His Word, we are carrying His Name
in vain.

CHAPTER 1

WHAT ARE YOU DOING WITH HIS NAME?

#Don'tLeaveHomeWithoutIt

Exodus, chapter twenty, verse seven says, "You shall not take the Name of the LORD your God in vain, for the LORD will not hold him guiltless who takes His Name in vain" (Exodus 20:7).

In 1975, American Express launched a very successful advertising campaign that ran from the mid-1970s to the late 1990s. The famous "Don't Leave Home Without It" tagline, which became synonymous with American Express Travelers Cheques, went on to become one of the most successful advertising campaigns of all time, and was such a success that it was relaunched in 2005.

The ads featured a number of famous faces who began by asking the viewer, "Do you know me?" The point was that although being famous might not have gotten those celebrities everything they wanted without having to pay, being a member of American Express would definitely get it for you.

Just like those American Express Travelers Cheques could get the desired result for the bearers of that currency, the Name of the Lord will guarantee results for its bearers, so long as they bear it with purpose, *and* expectation, *and* intentionality, *and* faith, *and* the like. American Express cautioned its bearers "not to leave home without it." Likewise, believers are commanded not to bear the Name of our Lord in vain, which begs the question for the title of this chapter, "What Are You Doing with His Name? #Don'tLeaveHomeWithoutIt."

"You shall not take the Name of the Lord your God in vain" is number three on the list of Ten Commandments that God gave Moses for His people after God delivered them from bondage in Egypt.

Cecil B DeMille captured this account in his classic film, *The Ten Commandments*, which starred Charlton Heston as Moses and Yul Brynner as the great Rameses. While Hollywood steered a good part of the movie away from true Scripture in order to yield the entertainment value that they sought, the film nevertheless does a good job of chronicling the life of Moses and of depicting the great Exodus, in which God used Moses to bring His people out of Egypt, out of the house of bondage, and through the wilderness in route to the Promised Land.

One of the most dramatic highlights in the movie has Moses standing high on the bank of the Red Sea with his staff raised above his head as the waters of the sea stand up on either side of the people, allowing them to march between those walls of water across the sea on dry ground.

Another great highlight of the film captures Aaron's creation of the golden calf under pressure from the people, and the people's riotous celebration over this calf, which they gave the credit for bringing them out of Egypt.

There are a lot of funny things that are captured in the Bible, but one of my favorites is what happened when Moses confronted Aaron about making that golden calf: Aaron lied through his teeth.

The Bible says that when the people asked Aaron to make them an idol god to worship, *Aaron* instructed them to give him their gold. The Bible says that *he* took that gold, *he* fashioned it with an engraving tool, and *he* made them a molded calf to worship. But when Moses asked Aaron what happened, and what was wrong with him, and why he did it, Aaron lied and said, "I [just] cast [the gold] into the fire, and this calf came out" (see Exodus 32:21-24; hereinafter, brackets mine).

God was so offended by this turn of the people that He said to Moses, "I am going to wipe them out and start all over with you." But Moses intervened, interceded, and stood in the gap for the people. And Moses tugged at the heartstrings of God for mercy.

Moses said, "Yes, Lord, this is a hard-headed stiff-necked people, but, Lord, You can't cut them off like that." Moses said, "Yes, Lord, they are fickle and wishy-washy, but You can't wipe them out like that." Moses said, "It will mess up Your reputation." He said, "The Egyptians will say that You just brought them out here into this wilderness to kill them."

And the Bible says that God backed up and relented from the harm that He was about to do. His mercy endures forever!

And so God brings the people out of Egypt and works great miracles on their behalf, and en route to the Promised Land, God gives them the Ten Commandments.

Now at a glance, when you go through the list of these Ten Commandments, they seem, for the most part, to be pretty straightforward: don't have any other god; don't make any images or serve any idols; keep the Sabbath day holy; honor your parents; don't kill; don't commit adultery;

#Don'tLeaveHomeWithoutIt

don't steal; don't bear false witness; don't covet (see Exodus 20:1-17).

But if you take a second glance, the third commandment, which is found in verse seven, is not so clear: in the New King James Version, that verse reads as follows: "You shall not take the Name of the LORD your God in vain" (Exodus 20:7).

Huh? What on earth does that mean? What does it mean to "take the Name?" And what does it mean to do so "in vain?"

Just like many of you, I grew up in church. And just like many of you, I have heard this taught. And just like many of you, I have heard two generally accepted explanations of this commandment.

The first is that we are not to profane the Name of the Lord by using it in cursing or in hostility.

To illustrate, that would suggest that we are not to say things like, "That G-D so-and-so is getting on my blankety-blank nerves." This is one illustration of what we were told it would look like to utter the Name of the Lord in vain, and this is an illustration of something we were therefore instructed not to do.

The second explanation that I have heard is that we are not to utter the Name of the Lord flippantly or disrespectfully or for the purpose of exclamation or emphasis.

This, for example, would suggest that we are not to say things like, "Jesus Christ, man! When are you guys going to finish the task?" This is another illustration of what we were told it means to utter the Name of the Lord in vain.

Now I absolutely agree that we are not to utter the Name of the Lord in cursing or in hostility. I absolutely agree that we should not say "G-D-it" and "blankety-blank." But while I absolutely agree that this should not be our practice, I do not believe that is what this commandment is talking about.

I also absolutely agree that we are not to utter the Name of the Lord flippantly or disrespectfully or for the purpose of exclamation or emphasis. I absolutely agree that we should not say things like, "Jesus Christ, will you shut up? You are getting on my nerves!" But while I absolutely agree that it should not be our practice to utter His Name in that manner, those barely scratch the surface of what this commandment is talking about.

"You shall not take the Name of the LORD your God in vain, for the LORD will not hold him guiltless who takes His Name in vain" (Exodus 20:7).

Our English translations of this scripture say, "You shall not *take* the Name of the Lord your God in vain." They do not say, "You shall not *utter* the Name of the Lord your God in vain."

When we interpret that scripture to mean "don't say things like, 'G-D-it, you can kiss my grits,'" we are interpreting it as "you shall not *utter* the Name of the Lord your God in an *irreverent* way. And though I agree that we should not utter His Name in that way, that is not what this scripture is saying.

When we interpret that scripture to mean "don't say things like 'Jesus Christ, I wish you would leave me alone,'" we are interpreting it as "you shall not *utter* the Name of the Lord your God in an *irreverent* way. And though I agree that we should not utter His Name in that way, that is not what this scripture is saying.

The correct interpretation of this scripture turns on what is meant by the word "take." You shall not "take" the Name of the Lord your God...

The Hebrew word is נָשָׂא (*nasa*), which means to "lift," "bear up," "carry," "take."

This Hebrew word *nasa'* is speaking about the action of lifting or lifting up, or hoisting something, like lifting weights or lifting up a baby from the car seat. If we were to inject this understanding here, it would say, "You shall not lift up the Name of the Lord your God in vain."

This word *nasa'* means to "bear," or "transport," or "move," like a police officer is authorized to bear arms, or like when Jesus had to bear His own cross until Simon of Cyrene showed up to bear it for Him. If we were to inject this understanding here, it would say, "You shall not bear the Name of the Lord your God in vain."

This word *nasa'* means to "carry" or "tote," which is to support and move (someone or something) from one place to another. It would be like a soldier who carries a wounded fellow soldier out of harm's way to a place of safety. In other words, this is saying, "You shall not carry or tote the Name of the Lord your God in vain."

This word *nasa'* means to "take," "take away," "carry off," "lay hold of (something) with one's hands," like "he took her hand and led her across the street." In other words, this is saying, "You shall not lay hold of the Name of the Lord your God in vain."

So one way to think of this word *nasa'* would be to get a picture of lifting up or hoisting His Name high in the air and carrying it around as a resource that you take everywhere you go to get what you need. Like American Express—don't leave home without it.

Thus, when this scripture says, "You shall not take the Name of the Lord your God in vain," it is not merely talking about *how you utter* His Name; it is talking about *what you do with* His Name. This passage is speaking to our purposefulness. This passage is speaking to our intent. This passage is speaking to our understanding of what the Name is and what the Name is for.

You shall not lift, bear up, carry, take the Name in vain. This is speaking to whether we really know what we have in our possession. This is speaking to whether we really know what we have in our midst.

That bodybuilder does not lift or hoist those weights in vain. He knows what those weights will do. And he knows how to use them to pump up.

That marine in a war is not bearing his firearm in vain; it is not there for decoration. If he hast to pull the trigger, it is not to wound. He is shooting to kill.

When you go grocery shopping and BYOB, you are not carrying those bags in vain. You intend to fill those bags with some groceries and bring those groceries from one place to another.

That parent who takes that child by the hand as they cross the street is not trying to be "touchy-feely." That parent is trying to get that child safely across the street.

Yes, it is true that we ought not to utter the Name of the Lord to curse people out. And yes, it is true that we ought not to utter the Name of the Lord to express our irritation or excitement. But this commandment is talking about a whole lot more than that.

This passage of Scripture is talking about knowing how to use the Name of the Lord to get you from point A to point B. This passage of Scripture is talking about knowing how to use the Name of the Lord to get you the results you need. This passage of Scripture is talking about knowing how to use the Name of the Lord to get your body healed. This passage of Scripture is talking about knowing how to use the Name of the Lord to get your needs met. This passage of Scripture is talking about knowing how to use the Name of

#Don'tLeaveHomeWithoutIt

the Lord to get the devil out of your household and off of your children. What are you doing with His Name?

If you are a believer, whether you know it or not, you take His Name with you everywhere you go. We are commanded not to take the Name of the Lord our God in vain. So the question is, what are you doing with His Name?

"The Name of the Lord is a strong tower;
The righteous run to it and are safe"
(Proverbs 18:10).

If you need a refuge, there is safety in His
   Name.
If you need a fix, there is power in His
   Name.
If you are in trouble, there is deliverance
   in His Name.
Even if you don't realize it, you've got His
   Name.
You shall not take the Name of the Lord
   your God in vain.
Don't leave home without it.

When you take His Name, you take His
   power.
When you take His Name, you take His
   presence.
When you take His Name, you take His
   Spirit.
Don't leave home without it.

Demons tremble at that Name.
Death succumbs to that Name.

DR. MELVIN G. BARNEY, ESQ.

There is deliverance in that Name.
What are you doing with His Name?

There is power in that Name.
There is authority in that Name.
Miracles are found in that Name.
Don't leave home without it.

Blinded eyes are opened in that Name.
Deaf ears are unstopped in that Name.
Muted tongues are loosed in that Name.
What are you doing with His Name?

The lame are made to walk in that Name.
Deformed limbs are repaired in that Name.
Blessings are released in that Name.
Don't leave home without it.

The question is: what are you doing with His Name?
You've got access to that Name. "You shall not take the Name
of the Lord your God in vain!"

CHAPTER 2

DON'T WASTE HIS NAME

#ThereIsSomethingAboutThatName

Now Peter and John went up together to the temple at the hour of prayer, the ninth hour. And a certain man lame from his mother's womb was carried, whom they laid daily at the gate of the temple which is called Beautiful, to ask alms from those who entered the temple; who, seeing Peter and John about to go into the temple, asked for alms. And fixing his eyes on him, with John, Peter said, "Look at us." So he gave them his attention, expecting to receive something from them. Then Peter said, "Silver and gold I do not have, but what I do have I give you: In the Name of Jesus Christ of Nazareth, rise up and walk." And he took him by the right hand and lifted him up, and immediately his feet and ankle bones received strength. So he, leaping

up, stood and walked and entered the
temple with them—walking, leaping,
and praising God. [...] Now as the lame
man who was healed held on to Peter and
John, all the people ran together to them
in the porch which is called Solomon's,
greatly amazed. So when Peter saw it, he
responded to the people: "Men of Israel,
why do you marvel at this? Or why look
so intently at us, as though by our own
power or godliness we had made this man
walk? [...] And His Name, through faith
in His Name, has made this man strong,
whom you see and know. Yes, the faith
which comes through Him has given him
this perfect soundness in the presence of
you all.

Acts 3:1-8, 11-12, 16

I can remember times when I was a kid: I had a really good
friend who came from a large family. Dinnertime at their
house reminded you of a scene from *Wild Kingdom*, where a
gang of vultures or hyenas or sharks were engaged in a feed-
ing frenzy.

Whenever they would have me over for dinner, I remember watching how my friend would pile up his plate with
much more than he could eat. I would watch as he picked
through the food on his plate, almost playing with it, until
he'd gotten enough.

And then I would watch as he tossed most of the food
that he'd piled on the plate into the trash. I remember thinking, *My mother would slaughter me if I were to waste food like*

that. He was wasting something that could have been put to good use somewhere else.

The other day I was watching a news report about the domino effect of this "new normal" from the pandemic. I watched as they discussed the impact on the economy, the record layoffs, the rise in food costs, and the increased demand on food banks. I was stunned by the images of people in lines that stretched out for several blocks, waiting for hours at a time, to be handed a box with a loaf of bread, some rice, and a few other staples that may last their families for three or four days.

As I think about these stories, I am blown away by the fact that this is not talking about what is happening abroad, in Africa, or in Guatemala, or in Haiti; this is talking about what is happening right here in our own backyard.

And so this news report was talking about how, on the one hand, people are pulling up to food banks and standing in food lines in record numbers, while on the other hand, many of the nation's dairy farmers are dumping out milk by the thousands of gallons because the restaurants and schools that are down their supply chains are closed on account of the regulations. And instead of finding a way to make good use of it, they dump it. What a waste!

You've got tens of thousands of people standing in these food lines, who could use the milk *and* butter *and* cheese that is being thrown out, literally poured down the drain, or dumped in a field, and wasted.

Fortunately, some agencies stepped in to broker a deal where the farmers could donate these dairy products to food banks instead of wasting them.

Waste is defined as "the failure to make good use of something." When something has value but is not being

#ThereIsSomethingAboutThatName

taken advantage of, that's waste. When something has value but is not being utilized, that's waste.

And so here, the message for the believer is, "Don't Waste My Name." #ThereIsSomethingAboutThatName.

Our reference scripture says, "You shall not take the Name of the Lord your God in vain." In the last chapter, we looked at what is meant by the phrase: "Take the Name of the Lord in vain." And we talked about two generally accepted interpretations of this phrase.

We pointed out that the first generally accepted interpretation is that we are not to profane the Name of the Lord by uttering His Name in cursing or in hostility, by saying things like, "G-D-it, I wish you would leave me the 'h-e-double-hockey-sticks' alone." The second generally accepted explanation that we hear is that we are not to utter the Name of the Lord flippantly or disrespectfully or for the purpose of exclamation or emphasis, by saying things like, "Jesus Christ! You need to just tell them how you feel."

While those are no doubt misuses of the Name of the Lord, the third commandment has little to do with uttering the Name irreverently. Instead, the correct interpretation of Exodus, chapter twenty, verse seven, turns on what is meant by the word "take." You shall not "take" the Name of the Lord your God in vain.

This is talking about how you "transport," "lift," "hoist up," "carry," or "bear" the Lord's Name. We are being strongly admonished not to "take" His Name around with us "in vain."

This brings me to what I want to focus on for the balance of this chapter: I want to focus on the phrase "in vain." "You shall not carry the Name of the Lord your God around with you *in vain*."

What does He mean by "in vain" or "vanity?" Well, one way of defining vain is "conceit or arrogance." So, for example, when you say, "She is so conceited," that's vanity. Or when you say, "He is very arrogant," that's one way of defining vanity.

However, in this context, the words "vain" and "vanity" are not dealing with the issues of conceit or arrogance. They are not talking about people with the "big head" who think they are "all that and a bag of chips." They are not talking about people who are in love with themselves and overly immersed in their own pride.

And when you think of it, that wouldn't even make sense. To say, "You shall not lift up the Name of the Lord your God in conceit or in arrogance" does not even make sense. This is not the definition of "vain" or "vanity" that applies here.

When we take a look at this in the Hebrew text, the Hebrew word is שָׁוְא (*shav*), which is here translated as "in vain," but which actually means:

> wastefully,
> uselessly,
> worthlessly,
> to no good purpose.

So, what He's actually saying is this: "You shall not take up the Name of the Lord your God wastefully." Instead, He wants you to take up the Name of the Lord your God economically so that you get good mileage out of it.

When He commands us not to take the Name of the Lord in vain, what He's telling us is, "You shall not lift up the Name of the Lord your God in a way that renders it useless."

Instead, He wants you to lift up the Name of the Lord your God in a way that renders it useful, useable, or valuable.

When He commands us not to take the Name of the Lord in vain, what He's telling us is, "You shall not bear the Name of the Lord your God in a worthless manner." Instead, He is instructing us to bear the Name of the Lord our God in a fruitful, or effective, or productive manner.

When He commands us not to take the Name of the Lord in vain, what He's telling us is, "You shall not carry the Name of the Lord your God to no good purpose." Instead, He is commanding us to carry the Name of the Lord our God with purpose and intentionality, having goals and results in mind.

It was a waste of good resources for my friend to pile up all of that food on his plate that he would ultimately throw in the trash and not eat. It was careless. It was to no purpose. It was not a good use of all the food that he tossed.

It was also a waste of good resources for those dairy farmers to dump out those thousands of gallons of milk when they could have donated it to the food banks and put it to good use to feed the thousands of people who were standing in the food bank lines. It was not prudent. It was to no purpose. It was not a good use of all the milk that they poured down the drain.

And it is likewise a waste of a good resource for the people of God to have the Name of the Lord available to us but not use that Name to deal with the things in our lives that are contrary to the Word of God.

It is like having a plate of food that you toss in the trash even though you or some others in your household are hungry.

It is like pouring out all of those tens of thousands of gallons of milk in the drain when you could supply thousands of hungry people with milk, *and* butter, *and* cheese, *and* ice cream.

And it would be like carrying an umbrella around with you, but not using it when it starts to rain. It is pouring down, raining. You are getting drenched. You have an umbrella in your hand. But you don't use it. What's wrong with you? It is a waste.

Acts, chapter three, verses one through five, states:

> Now Peter and John went up together to the temple at the hour of prayer, the ninth hour. And a certain man lame from his mother's womb was carried, whom they laid daily at the gate of the temple which is called Beautiful, to ask alms from those who entered the temple; who, seeing Peter and John about to go into the temple, asked for alms. And fixing his eyes on him, with John, Peter said, "Look at us." So he gave them his attention, expecting to receive something from them.

Then Peter said, "Silver and gold I do not have, but what I do have I give you: In the Name of Jesus…"

I'm talking about the Name that is the Name above every Name.

It's in that Name that every knee shall bow and that every tongue shall confess.

It's in that Name that we can ask for things with the expectation that whatever we ask will be given.

Peter said, "Silver and gold I do not have, but what I do have I give you: In the Name of Jesus Christ of Nazareth, rise up and walk."

#ThereIsSomethingAboutThatName

Beginning from verse six, the Bible says:

> Then Peter said, "Silver and gold I do not
> have, but what I do have I give you: In the
> Name of Jesus Christ of Nazareth, rise up
> and walk." And he took him by the right
> hand and lifted him up, and immediately
> his feet and ankle bones received strength.
> So he, leaping up, stood and walked and
> entered the temple with them—walking,
> leaping, and praising God. [...] Now as
> the lame man who was healed held on
> to Peter and John, all the people ran
> together to them in the porch which is
> called Solomon's, greatly amazed. So
> when Peter saw it, he responded to the
> people: "Men of Israel, why do you mar-
> vel at this? Or why look so intently at us,
> as though by our own power or godliness
> we had made this man walk? [...] And
> His Name, through faith in His Name,
> has made this man strong, whom you
> see and know. Yes, the faith which comes
> through Him has given him this perfect
> soundness in the presence of you all.
>
> Acts 3:6-8, 11-12, 16

It's in the Name. There is something about that Name. Peter said, "Don't look at me like I am so wonderful. It's the Name. Don't look at me in admiration. It's the Name." He said, "Silver and gold, I have none. But I have something greater: I've got the Name. I did not bring my checkbook with me today, but I've got the Name. I forgot my wallet today, but I've got the Name. Silver and gold, I have none. But what I do have, I give you: In the Name of Jesus Christ of Nazareth…" It's in the Name.

Don't waste that Name.

There is something about that Name. Don't waste it.

It is a waste of God's Name for the believer to take it around like an umbrella but not use it when we see our brother or sister struggling with sickness and disease. That's taking His Name in vain. Don't waste His Name.

It is a waste of God's Name for us to carry it like an umbrella but not use it when we see our children and grand-children tied up by the devil. That's carrying His Name in vain. Don't waste His Name.

It is a waste of God's Name for us to carry it like an umbrella but not use it when we see the enemy trying to stir up a bunch of confusion and strife and bickering and back-biting in our midst. That's toting His Name around in vain. Don't waste His Name.

It is a waste of God's Name for us to bear it like an umbrella but not use it when we are walking around in dis-tress, or bondage, or depression. That's bearing His Name in vain. Don't waste His Name.

It is a waste of God's Name for us to lift it like an umbrella but not use it when we cannot pay our bills, even though we are in covenant with the One Who has made us the head and not the tail. That's lifting up His Name in vain. Don't waste His Name.

You shall not take the Name of the Lord your God in vain. What are you doing with His Name? Don't waste His Name.

Jesus said you can cast out devils in His Name. You see that devil trying to take over your household? Cast him out. Don't waste His Name.

#ThereIsSomethingAboutThatName

27

Jesus said you can lay hands on the sick, and they will recover, in His Name. You don't have to accept that negative report from the doctor. Lay hands on your child, in His Name. Lay hands on your spouse, in His Name. Lay hands on your mother, in His Name. Lay hands on yourself, in His Name. Don't waste His Name.

Jesus said you can ask for miracles, in His Name. Don't be discouraged. Pick yourself up. Ask the Lord to work that thing out, in His Name. Don't you dare give up. Ask the Lord for the power to overcome, in His Name. Don't back down. Ask the Lord for the miracles that you need, in His Name. Don't waste His Name.

You shall not take the Name of the Lord your God in vain. What are you doing with His Name? Don't waste His Name.

Jesus said, "Whatever you ask the Father in My Name, He will give it to you." What are you asking the Father to do in Jesus's Name?

You shall not take the Name of the Lord your God in vain. Don't Waste His Name.

CHAPTER 3

SAY MY NAME

#YourPowerOfAttorney

The fifteenth chapter of the Gospel, according to St. John, reads as follows:

> You did not choose Me, but I chose you and appointed you that you should go and bear fruit, and that your fruit should remain, that whatever you ask the Father in My Name He may give you.
>
> John 15:16

The other day I was watching an advertisement that was promoting the music from the '60s, including some of the singles released by Diana Ross & the Supremes. As I started researching some of the lyrics, I could not help but take note of some of the changes in the way the ladies back then confronted certain "relationship challenges," as compared to how they do that today.

Back then, for example, in "Stop! In The Name of Love," Diana Ross speaks of knowing where her "baby" goes and who he meets when he leaves her side. She tells him about the pain it causes her and asks him to think about how good she has been to him. In "Baby Love," she reflects on how much she needs him, asks why he treats her so bad and leaves her so sad, and questions what she did wrong. In "You Keep Me Hangin' On," she begs him to set her free and leave her alone since he obviously doesn't really want her but keeps playing with her heart.

If Diana Ross & The Supremes are the model for how ladies of the '60s confronted these types of "relationship issues," oh, how times have changed!

As representatives of the ladies of the twenty-first century, Beyonce Knowles and Kelly Rowland, and the group Destiny's Child present a different approach for addressing these so-called "relationship challenges."

In "Say My Name, Say My Name," Beyonce points out that her boyfriend's conduct is suspicious, his conversations have become very cryptic, he's acting "kinda shady," and if he has been unfaithful, she is not having it. She lets him know that she does not trust him, she is not going to be "played," and if he wants to prove to her that he is not cheating on her, then without hesitation, he needs to "say her name."

The title for this chapter is "Say My Name! #YourPowerofAttorney."

I need to point out here that Beyonce and Kelly and Destiny's Child had their reasons for making the demands that this guy said her name, just as God has His reasons for demanding that we say His Name. As for Beyonce, she made it very clear that she wasn't playing and that she wasn't "going to be played." God, likewise, makes it clear that He is not playing around, but He instructs us to say His Name for a different reason and a different purpose.

Unlike Beyonce, God is not trying to check us or trap us or ensnare us. However, God *is* trying to show us how to make things happen. God *is* trying to teach us the route to victory. And God *is* trying to set us up for the blessing—by the use of His Name.

God wants us to recognize the power that is available to us, in His Name. God wants us to recognize that He has given us authority to use His Name. And God wants us to be purposeful, *and* intentional, *and* deliberate in the use of His Name.

As children of God, as the people of God, and as agents of God, we have been given authority to carry the Name of the Lord around with us in order to shake up some things in the spiritual realm and cause things to manifest in the natural realm. As children of God, we have the authority to tote His Name around with us in order to rattle the devil's cage. As children of God, we've got the authority to transport His Name around with us in order to change the status quo.

The message that God wants to get across to His people is that we have been given the power of attorney to do things and act, in His Name.

> You did not choose Me, but I chose you
> and appointed you that you should go
> and bear fruit, and that your fruit should
> remain, that whatever you ask the Father
> in My [N]ame He may give you.
> John 15:16

God wants us to "bear fruit." Because He wants us to bear fruit, He has instructed us to ask for whatever we will need in order to bear that fruit. And to guarantee us that we will be heard, to guarantee that we will get through, to guar-

#YourPowerOfAttorney

antee that we will be provided with whatever we need to bear that fruit, He says, "Just ask in My Name, and you will get whatever you want." That's a power of attorney.

What Is a Power of Attorney?

A power of attorney is a legal authorization to act on someone else's behalf. For example, you might have a power of attorney to manage someone else's property, or handle another person's finances, or conduct someone's business affairs, or make medical decisions on behalf of another person. If someone has given you legal authority to act on his or her behalf, that is the conferment of a power of attorney.

A few things to note about powers of attorney:

1. Powers of attorney are fully enforceable by law. Not discretionary. Not debatable.
2. Powers of attorney can be broad. Example: all affairs.
3. Powers of attorney can be specific or narrow. Example: medical decisions.

The person who grants a power of attorney has the right to determine its scope, its limitations, whether it will be broad, whether it will be narrow.

When you give someone a power of attorney, you are authorizing that person to act on your behalf. And when someone gives you a power of attorney, they are giving you the legal authority to act on their behalf.

Here, in this passage of Scripture, Jesus granted us the power of attorney to act on His behalf. In John chapter fifteen, verse sixteen, He suggests, "I have an agenda. I need you to bear fruit. I need your fruit to remain." And so, He points out that in order to facilitate this, "whatever you need in order to bear fruit, God will give it to you—as long as you present your power of attorney, which is 'The Name.'"

Someone may wonder, what is this business about bearing fruit? What is He talking about? When He speaks of bearing fruit, He is talking about an assortment of things. He is talking about obeying His Word. He is talking about whatever you find in the Bible. He is talking about walking in the authority He has given you. He is talking about living a victorious life. He is talking about doing the things He did and working the works He worked. He is talking about receiving the manifestation of the promise. Jesus said, "I am the vine, you are the branches" (John 15:5). So the fruit that the branches bear would be the same fruit that grows on the vine.

Thus, in order to enable us to do this and bear the same fruit that He bore, Jesus conferred upon us the power of attorney.

If you ever had a power of attorney to act on someone's behalf, you probably know that it is the power of attorney that gets the results, not you. You probably know that it is the power of attorney that gets the job done, not you.

If you go to the bank and try to withdraw from Joe Jones's account without a power of attorney, they just might escort you out of the bank. You have to present the power of attorney.

If you take Susie Smith's checkbook and try to write a check to purchase an expensive piece of jewelry for her without a power of attorney, they just might arrest you. You have to present the power of attorney.

Thus, the power is in the power of attorney, not you. Let me repeat that: the power is in the power of attorney.

#YourPowerOfAttorney

The Power Is in the Name

Jesus said, "I have given you My Name," and the power is in the Name.

It is as if God is saying, "Please, don't get it twisted." It is not because you are a great wonder, and a great wonder I know you are, but the power is in the Name. I know that you are well-connected, but it is not because you are so popular. The power is in the Name. I know that you are super smart, but it is not because you are an intellectual genius. The power is in the Name. I know that you are influential and charming, but it really has nothing to do with your influence, and it has nothing to do with your charm. The power is in the Name. It's not about how stylish you dress, or how primpy you are, or whether you comb your hair to the front or to the back, or about the fact that those eyelashes are bigger than your face. The power is in the Name.

> Then the seventy returned with joy, saying, "Lord, even the demons are subject to us in Your Name." And He said to them, "I saw Satan fall like lightning from heaven. Behold, I give you the authority to trample on serpents and scorpions, and over all the power of the enemy, and nothing shall by any means hurt you."
>
> Luke 10:17-19

The power is in the Name. You shall not take the Name of the Lord your God in vain. The power is in the Name, and you've got the authority to use it. Whenever the devil starts cutting up, you can whip out that Name. Whenever the devil starts getting on your nerves, you can bring out that Name.

DR. MELVIN G. BARNEY, ESQ.

Whenever the devil starts trying you, you can lift up the Name. God says, "You need to stop running from the devil and instead, say My Name. You need to stop whining about all that he is doing and instead, say My Name. You need to stop bragging about how good a job the devil is doing and instead, say My Name."

Jesus said, "I was there. I saw Satan kicked out of heaven. I saw the devil stripped of his power. He has no more authority over you." "Behold, I give you the authority to trample on serpents and scorpions, and over all the power of the enemy, and nothing shall by any means hurt you" (Luke 10:19). It's in the Name. Jesus says, "Say *My* Name, say *My* Name."

He Is the Vine; We Are the Branches

> I am the vine, you are the branches. He who abides in Me, and I in him, bears much fruit; for without Me you can do nothing. If anyone does not abide in Me, he is cast out as a branch and is withered; and they gather them and throw them into the fire, and they are burned. If you abide in Me, and My [W]ords abide in you, you will ask what you desire, and it shall be done for you.
>
> John 15:5-7

Jesus wants us to be clear that *He* is the vine. We are not the vine. We are the branches. As was His custom, Jesus taught spiritual concepts by the use of parables, allegories, and word pictures. In this illustration, He makes it clear that while clusters of grapes may be found to grow directly from the branches that sprout from a grapevine, the branches must

#YourPowerOfAttorney

necessarily be connected to that vine in order to bear the fruit or grapes.

In the natural, as long as the branch of a grapevine is connected to the vine, it can bear grapes. Likewise, as long as the branch of an apple tree is connected to the trunk of that tree, it can bear apples. Why? The answer is circular. They can respectively bear fruit *because* the branch of the grapevine is connected to its vine and *because* the branch of the apple tree is connected to its tree trunk. In the case of the grapevine, the vine is the source of life for the branches of the grapevine; and in the case of the apple tree, the trunk is the source of life for the branches of the apple tree. If you disconnect a branch from its vine or its trunk, it will die because you have cut off its life source.

Jesus uses this word picture to let us know that He *does* want us to bear fruit, just as the owner of a grapevine wants to see clusters of grapes growing on his vines and just as the owner of an apple tree wants to see juicy apples growing on his apple trees. But Jesus also wants it to be clear to us that our ability to bear fruit is tied to our connection to Him and that the only way we can bear fruit is if we remain connected to Him.

In other words, it's not about us. It's all about Him. Just as the power to transact business on behalf of another is not in the agent, but in the power of attorney, our ability to bear fruit is not in or of ourselves or our greatness, but it is because of *Him*.

Jesus said, "You have not chosen me, I chose you." His point is, "I have an agenda. And in order for Me to accomplish My agenda, you need to bear fruit. I did not save you, so you can sit around and look pretty. You need to bear fruit." Jesus is saying, "I did not pull you up out of the muck and the mire so that you can look down your nose at somebody else who is struggling. You need to win souls." Jesus is saying, "I did not work that miracle in your life so you could run around and try to impress people. You need to get somebody healed." Jesus is saying, "I did not deliver you from that disgusting slush that you were sloshing around in, so you could sit back and look important. You need to get somebody delivered."

> You did not choose Me, but I chose you and appointed you that you should go and bear fruit, and that your fruit should remain, that whatever you ask the Father in My Name He may give you.
>
> John 15:16

So, when Beyonce and Kelly said, "Say my name, say my name," they were talking about one thing. But when Jesus says, "Say My Name, Say My Name," He is talking about something altogether different.

When Beyonce was telling you, "Say my name," she was talking about busting you out. But when Jesus was telling you, "Say My Name," He was talking about raising you up. When Kelly Rowland was telling you, "Say my name," she was talking about exposing you. But when Jesus was telling you, "Say My Name," He was talking about defeating your enemy. When Destiny's Child was telling you, "Say my name," they were talking about tripping you and trapping you. But when Jesus was telling you, "Say My Name," He was talking about giving you the victory.

"Say My Name, say My Name." The power of attorney is in His Name. You have all that power at your disposal. Just "Say My Name." Whatever you ask, just "Say My Name." Whatever you need, just "Say My Name." Somebody's healing is right there in your mouth, just "Say My Name."

#YourPowerOfAttorney

Somebody's breakthrough is at the tip of your tongue, just "Say My Name."

God is saying, "I have given you the power of attorney. Whatever you ask in My Name, I will do it." You shall not carry the Name of the Lord your God in vain. "Say My Name, say My Name."

CHAPTER 4

USE THE NAME AS A TOOL

#You'dBetterRecognize

For this next section of our teaching, let's go over to the four-teenth chapter of the Gospel according to St. John, which reads as follows: "And whatever you ask in My Name, that I will do, that the Father may be glorified in the Son. If you ask anything in My Name, I will do it" (John 14:13-14).

In the last chapter, we talked about the power of attorney that Jesus has conveyed to us through the use of His Name.

We have been authorized to make requests in the Name of Jesus, and when we do so, the devil has to back down and let go of our belongings, whether he wants to or not.

You can tell the devil to loose your body or get out of your finances or leave your children alone, in the Name of Jesus. And whether he likes it or not, he will have to turn your body loose and leave your harvest alone and release your children because your power of attorney is vested in the Name of Jesus.

We have the power of attorney in the Name of Jesus, and therefore, whatever we bind on earth, God will bind in heaven; and whatever we loose on earth, God will loose in heaven.

And so, for this chapter, I want to talk about using your power of attorney as a tool to get what God has promised you.

If I go into the bank and try to make a $1 million withdrawal on Chandler Bing's behalf, the only reason the bank would be required to give me the money is because I have a power of attorney. And after I fill out the withdrawal slip, when I get to the teller window, the teller will ask me to show some ID. If I only show her my California Driver's License, the teller might look at me and say, "One moment, please," while she pushes that little button to call the police. But if I bust out the power of attorney that Chandler Bing has given me, her response will change, and now she will smile at me and say, "Welcome to Bank of America; how may I help you?"

Thus, it was the power of attorney that enabled me to get the money. It was the power of attorney that got me the result.

If I had not produced the power of attorney and just said, "But Chandler Bing needs me to help her manage her money," that teller would have said, "One moment, please," while she pressed that little button.

If I had said, "Do you know who I am? I have an MBA from Carnegie Mellon University, a Juris Doctorate from University of California, Los Angeles, and a Doctorate on Ministry from United Theological Seminary." She would have just said, "One moment, please," and pressed that little button.

If I had said, "This is an outrage! I am her pastor, her man of God. And we go waaaaay back." The teller would have just said, "One moment, please," and pressed that little button.

DR. MELVIN G. BARNEY, ESQ.

There is only one way that teller would have allowed me to make the withdrawal and given me that money: I would have to demonstrate that I had been given the power of attorney. And if I did not have proof of it or if I did not use it, perhaps you guys would see me in 3–5 years, or they might let me out earlier for good behavior. Why? Because the authorization for me to go into Chandler Bing's bank and withdraw that $1 million is in the power of attorney.

Now, let's fast forward 3–5 years. (They didn't let me out for good behavior!) And let's say I go back into that bank and meet up again with that same teller. And let's say I try to withdraw $1 million this time from Madam X's account. (The first thing they would say is, "You are in the wrong bank. You are supposed to be at Wells Fargo.")

But let's say that after we get through all of that, the teller recognizes me from before. And with the same smirk on her face as before, she says, "One moment, please," and reaches down to press that button.

This time, if I learned anything from the previous incident, when she started to reach for that button, I would know that I need to bust out that power of attorney—so here it goes, *bam*! Because when I do that, when I produce the power of attorney that Madam X has given me, the teller's response will change, and now she will smile at me and say, "Welcome to Bank of America (or Wells Fargo), how may I help you?"

Therefore, it was the power of attorney that enabled me to get the money. It was the power of attorney that got me the result.

The last time this happened, 3–5 years ago, when it was Chandler Bing's account, I had a power of attorney, but because I did not use it, I did not get the result—even though I had a power of attorney. Again, because I did not *use* the

#You'dBetterRecognize

power of attorney that I had in my possession, I did not get the result that I sought, *even though I had a right to it.*

This time, with Madam X, I learned the lesson. I learned that if I want the result, I have got to use the power of attorney like it is a tool. Why? Because as great and wonderful as I may be, I need a power of attorney to get the result. It needs to click on the inside of me that a power of attorney is a tool that is necessary for me to get the result that I am going after.

In this chapter, I want to talk about using the Name as a tool.

When I look around our church, we are blessed to have an abundance of talent in our midst.

Anybody who knows anything about Rose F. knows that she is a master baker, who can not only bake you a cake that will make you want to "slap somebody's momma," but she is also an amazing cake designer and decorator and artist who can design that cake and decorate that cake and sculpt that cake into a masterpiece that looks too good to eat. Talent.

We also have a dynamic duo in our midst, Sylvia J. and Dorothy H., who are shopaholics in denial, but who can put you a meal together for you that is fit for a king.

Sylvia, who I call "Jack," truly knows how to "make a dollar out of fifteen cents." And Dorothy, who I call "Dottie Mae," can make boiled water taste like a gourmet meal! Talent.

We have Crawford J., Sonya J., Commander, Darice M., and Taylor J., who have been working very diligently at the church with some others as well, putting everything together that needs to be put together and assembling everything that needs to be assembled and setting up everything that needs to be set up. And when they finish whatever they are working on, it looks like it should be on exhibit in somebody's museum. Talent.

We've got Tony G. zipping through the place, checking out the wiring: climbing all up into the ceiling, rewiring what needs to be rewired, and putting in new wiring where there needs to be new wiring, and installing outlets where we need new outlets. Talent.

And then there is Uncle L., a Picasso on "a whole 'nother level." Whereas the real Pablo Picasso's canvas was something like a 3 × 4 piece of cardboard on an easel, Uncle L.'s canvas could be the interior or exterior walls of your house. Talent.

I don't have time to keep naming people, but there is no question that we have tons and tons of talent in our midst. But one thing I have noticed is that although they are the best of the best at what they do, and though they are the most talented of the talented at what they do, they cannot do what they do to the extent that they do it unless they have the right tools in hand. All talent needs their tools.

As much as you may want to "slap somebody's momma" when you bite into a slice of Rosie's cake, she cannot do a thing for you without an oven that will heat up to 350 degrees.

In order for Jack to "make a dollar out of fifteen cents," and in order for Dottie Mae to make that boiling water taste like something you would order from a five-star restaurant, they need some pots, some pans, and some Lawry's seasoned salt.

Crawford, Sonya, Commander, Darice, and Taylor had to bring some drills, screwdrivers, and hammers with them in order to assemble what they assembled and to repair what they repaired. But there were a few things that needed to be assembled and that needed to be repaired, which they were unable to assemble and repair—because those things required a drill bit or a screwdriver head that none of them had with them at the time.

#You'dBetterRecognize

Shortly after Tony revealed that he could run the wiring that we needed in order to hook up all of the electronics that we have, and when he said he would install the outlets and sockets that needed to be installed to ensure that we can plug up everything we need to plug up, he submitted a shopping list of the things that we would need to acquire, in order for him to be able to run the wiring that needs to be run and connect the sockets that need to be connected.

So as awesome and amazing and gifted as he is, Tony needs more than his awesomeness and amazingness and giftedness in order to get the job one. Why? Because all talent needs their tools.

I also noticed that while Uncle L. was in the church glazing those walls, and sprucing up those rooms, and cutting those edges, and making God's house look like a place that just might cause God to stand up from His throne and applaud, Uncle L. had brushes, and rollers, and paint, and ladders, and paint sprayers, and had to run back and forth to Home Depot several times to pick up the things that he needed to deck those halls with something other than boughs of holly.

No matter what we may bring to the table, whatever gifts and talents we have, no matter who we may know and what we may know, if we are going to get it done, we need the right tools. All talent needs their tools.

Recognize and Use the Name of the Lord as a Tool

Our foundation scripture tells us not to carry the Name of the Lord our God around with us in vain. If we are going to see the power of God fully at work in our midst, it is vital that we recognize the Name of the Lord as a tool, and it is vital that we use the Name of the Lord as a tool.

DR. MELVIN G. BARNEY, ESQ.

In our text, at verses thirteen and fourteen of John, chapter fourteen, the Scripture says, "And whatever you ask in My Name, that I will do, that the Father may be glorified in the Son. If you ask anything in My Name, I will do it."

You'd better recognize: God wants us to learn to use His Name as a tool.

Now let me just point this out: when you are operating in a power of attorney, you do not have to be coy or passive or shy or insecure. You can be bold and assertive and stern and confident because you already know what results that power of attorney is going to get for you.

Likewise, when you recognize the role your tools will play in getting you the results that you seek, you are not coy or passive or shy or insecure. You have an expectation. You know what results those tools are going to get you.

Uncle L. fully expects those rollers and brushes to affix that paint to the walls. Rosie fully expects that oven to bake that cake. Tony fully expects those crimper things to splice that wire. It is no surprise that the tools you need to do the job are able to deliver. You can always be confident that the tools you use are going to do their job.

Likewise, when we recognize that the Name of the Lord is our tool to get the promise of God to come to pass, we can be bold and assertive and stern and confident, because we know what His Name is going to accomplish for us.

When this scripture tells us to ask in Jesus's Name, there needs to be an expectation. When Rosie sets that oven to 350 degrees, she is not wondering if it will bake that cake. She is expecting it to bake that cake. When Uncle L. dipped that brush in the can of paint, he was not wondering if the brush could cause the paint to stick to the wall. He knew what it would do. There was an expectation.

#You'dBetterRecognize

Likewise, when Jesus tells us that He will do whatever we ask *in His Name,* we have to have an expectation. In this context, the word "ask" is not talking about being coy, passive, shy, or insecure. You have to be confident in your tool's ability to get you the results you seek.

Have Confidence in Your Tools

Let's examine what the Scripture means and what Jesus was talking about when He told us to "ask."

The Greek word is αἰτέω, and although it is translated as "ask," it means:

> demand,
> require,
> insist on,
> ask for in expectation of a response.

Even though it is translated as "ask" in John 14, Jesus is not talking about being coy or passive or shy or insecure. This word, αἰτέω, speaks of being bold and assertive and stern and confident.

Thus, what Jesus is saying in John, chapter fourteen, is this:

"Whatever you *demand* in My Name, that I will do, that the Father may be glorified in the Son. If you *demand* anything in My Name, I will do it." That's not coy; that's assertive.

"Whatever you *require* in My Name, that I will do, that the Father may be glorified in the Son. If you *require* anything in My Name, I will do it." That's not passive; that's bold.

"Whatever you *insist on* in My Name, that I will do, that the Father may be glorified in the Son. If you *insist on* anything in My Name, I will do it." That's not shy; that's stern.

"Whatever you *ask for in expectation of a response* in My Name, that I will do, that the Father may be glorified in the Son. If you *ask for* anything *in expectation of a response* in My Name, I will do it." That's not insecure; that's confident.

Just like Jack and Dottie Mae are confident that they can produce a five-star gourmet meal with those pots and pans and Lawry's seasoned salt, we have to be confident that demons will flee when we speak that Name.

And just like Crawford, Sonya, Commander, Darice, and Taylor have no doubt that they can assemble anything with the right screwdriver and drill, you have to be confident that that cancer has to go from your body when you speak that Name.

And just like Tony knows he can get the electricity flowing everywhere it is needed throughout the church if he has the items he needs, we have to be confident that the windows of heaven will open for us when we speak that Name.

We have to have confidence that our tools will get the job done.

We have to be confident that the promise will manifest when we speak that Name.

We have to be confident that the Name of the Lord is the tool God has given us to get the promised result.

John, chapter fourteen, verses thirteen and fourteen, says, "And whatever you ask in My Name, that I will do, that the Father may be glorified in the Son. If you ask anything in My Name, I will do it."

And verse seven of Exodus, chapter twenty, says, "You shall not take the Name of the LORD your God in vain, for

#You'dBetterRecognize

the LORD will not hold him guiltless who takes His Name in vain."

Don't carry His Name around with you in vain. You'd better recognize. Use it as a tool. Just like that oven will bake you a cake, and those pots will cook you a meal, use the Name of the Lord as a tool to get your deliverance.

Jesus said, "*Whatever* you ask *in My Name*, I will do it." You've got to use the Lord's Name as a tool. Just like you would use a screwdriver to assemble a bookcase and a hammer to nail two pieces of wood together, use the Name of Jesus as a tool to restore peace in your household. You'd better recognize!

Don't transport the Lord's Name to no avail. Use it as a tool. Just like a painter would use a ladder to reach the top of the wall and an angled brush to cut those corners, use the Name of the Lord as a tool to get your body healed. You'd better recognize!

"If you ask *anything in My Name*, I will do it." You'd better recognize! Use the Name of Jesus as a tool. Just like an electrician would use an electrician's fishing tool to run that cabling and some needle-nose pliers to cut and bend those wires, you have to use the Name of the Lord as a tool to get your breakthrough. You'd better recognize!

You shall not take the Name of the Lord your God in vain. Use the Name as a tool.

CHAPTER 5

SOW THE NAME AS A SEED

#HallowingHisName

We have been dissecting the third commandment not to take the Name of the Lord our God in vain and examining the power that is available to us in the Name of the Lord. God wants us to utilize His Name to defeat the enemy, and to work our miracles, and to shake up some things, and to bring about our deliverance, and to cause the promises of God to manifest in our lives.

For this chapter, let's go over to the Gospel according to St. Luke, the eleventh chapter, and look at verse two, which reads as follows: "So [Jesus] said to them, 'When you pray, say: Our Father in heaven, Hallowed be Your Name.'"

In Chapter 3, we talked about the power of attorney that Jesus has conveyed to us through the use of His Name. You have been authorized and even instructed to make requests and demands, in the Name of Jesus; and when you do so, the enemy has to let your belongings go, whether he wants to or not.

Because of your power of attorney, you can tell the devil to loose your body, in the Name of Jesus. You can tell the devil to release your finances, in the Name of Jesus. You can command that devil to leave your children alone, in the Name of Jesus. And the devil doesn't have to like it, or want to, or think highly of you, or respect you—because the power is in the Name. We have power of attorney, in the Name of Jesus. And the Bible says, whatever you bind on earth shall be bound in heaven. And whatever you loose on earth shall be loosed in heaven.

Accordingly, we need to learn to use the power of attorney that we have in His Name as a tool to get what God has promised us—in the same way that Rosie uses an oven to bake her cakes, and in the same way Jack and Dottie Mae use those pots & pans to prepare a gourmet meal, and in the same way Crawford and Sonya and Commander and Darice and Taylor use their screwdrivers to assemble furniture, and in the same way that Tony uses an electrician's fishing tool to run cabling, and in the same way that Uncle L. uses his rollers to paint walls. No matter how skilled, talented, and gifted you may be, you still need your tools to get the job done.

God said, "You shall not take the Name of the Lord your God in vain." Use it like you would use the oven. Use it like you would use a screwdriver.

We have to see the Name of the Lord as the tool that we need to use in order to get the promise to manifest. Use the Name.

We have talked about the power of attorney we have in His Name, and we have talked about using the Name of the Lord as a tool. Now, I want to go a little bit further and talk about using the Name of the Lord as a seed.

> And He said, "The kingdom of God is as if a man should scatter seed on the ground, and should sleep by night and rise by day, and the seed should sprout

and grow, he himself does not know how
[...] But when the grain ripens, immediately he puts in the sickle, because the
harvest has come."

Mark 4:26-29

According to this passage of Scripture, the kingdom of
God can be associated with seed. In other words, the sowing of seed is a kingdom principle. Lately, at our church, we
have been doing a lot of teaching on seed because God has
given us the revelation that this is one of the most important
principles that discloses how the kingdom of God operates.
And one of the fascinating things about seeds is that God put
within every seed the power to make itself come to pass.

In Genesis, chapter one, verse eleven, where we are introduced to the kingdom principle of seed, the Bible says, "Then
God said, 'Let the earth bring forth grass, the herb that yields
seed, and the fruit tree that yields fruit according to its kind,
whose seed is in itself, on the earth'; and it was so."

God put within every seed the power to make itself
come to pass.

But we have also talked about the fact that seeds have
to be planted if you expect them to grow. I can remember, as
a young kid, watching my grandmother masterfully manage
one of the largest gardens that I had ever seen anyone grow in
the city. My grandmother was from the south. And she was
used to having a huge garden in the south. You know how
they say, "You can take a person out of the country, but you
can't take the country out of that person?" When it comes to
gardening, I think they were talking about my grandmother.
She may have migrated from the rural south to the metro-
politan north, but it seemed that she had brought her garden
with her.

#HallowingHisName

I remember watching her on a daily basis messing around with her garden. She was constantly planting seeds, watering what was planted, pulling up weeds, and monitoring what was growing. As a part of her meal planning for the day, she would go out to her garden and bring back whatever vegetables and fruits she intended to use in the meals for the day.

I also remember how she had a practice of stockpiling packets of seed in her windowsills. Sometimes, the packets of seed would sit in her windowsill for months and maybe even a year or more before she used them. As long as those packets of seeds sat in my grandmother's windowsill, nothing happened. They just remained packets of seed that had turned brown from sitting in the windowsill for so long. But they did not produce anything.

Occasionally, my grandmother would go out to gather some vegetables and fruits from her garden and notice that she was low on green beans or had run out of cabbage, for example. All of a sudden, she would remember that she had some green bean seed and some cabbage seed in the windowsill. Often, she would tell my brother or me to go and grab certain packets of seed from that windowsill for her; and we would watch as she planted that seed in her garden. A few weeks or months later, she would have a flurry of green beans on several stalks in her garden, or we would find heads of cabbage by the rows in her garden.

As long as those packets of seed sat in the windowsill, they did not produce anything. But when my grandmother took the seed from the windowsill and planted it in the garden, she received the manifestation of what she had planted. The lesson is that seed has to be sown for it to produce a harvest, but it is guaranteed to produce, because God put the power in the seed to make itself come to pass (see Genesis

1:11-12). Nevertheless, if it is going to produce, the seed must be sown (see Mark 4:26-29).

Jesus said in Luke chapter eight, verse eleven, that God's Words are seeds. And just like any other seed, God's Words are the seed that contain within themselves the power to make themselves come to pass (see Genesis 1:11-12). This is a kingdom principle. Thus, since God's Words are seeds, God put the power in the Word to make itself come to pass.

But just like I have to sow tomato seeds if I want to see tomatoes grow, I have to sow *words* if I want to see them manifest.

So the question is, how do we sow words? How do we plant words? The way we plant our words is by speaking them.

In response to the query of His followers, Jesus said, "When you pray, *say*: Our Father in heaven, Hallowed be Your Name" (Luke 11:2, emphasis added). This passage is probably the best-known scripture of all time, and I would venture to say that you would be hard-pressed to cross paths with someone who has never heard of this prayer.

Here, Jesus told His followers to pray by *saying*, "Our Father in heaven, hallowed be Your Name." He is teaching His followers how to sow the Name of the Lord. The way you sow, or plant words, is by *speaking* them. Thus, words are our spiritual seeds.

With the understanding that words are your spiritual seed, there are a few things I want to point out:

1. Words are sown by speaking them. The way we sow spiritual seeds is by speaking words. It's not enough to think them. That's like having a packet of seed in your windowsill that you have not planted. Just like you have to plant that packet of seed to sow it, you have to speak the Words of God to sow them.

#HallowingHisName

2. When we speak God's Words, they will manifest themselves. All seeds produce after their own kind. God put the power in the seed to make itself come to pass. This is a kingdom principle. Likewise, God put the power in the words that we speak to make themselves come to pass.

3. When Jesus said, "When you pray, *say*: Our Father in heaven, Hallowed be Your Name" (emphasis added), He is teaching us to sow the Name of the Lord in order to extract from God's Name the *what* and the *Who* God promises to be for us. Why? Because God put within the seed the power to make itself come to pass. And God put within the spoken Word the power to make itself come to pass. And God put within the Name that we "hallow" the power to make itself come to pass.

Let's talk about how the kingdom of God operates with respect to sowing seed.

In the natural, if I have a taste for some apple cobbler (I know I am speaking to a lot of peach cobbler fans, but I love a good apple cobbler), so if I want some apple cobbler, I can either go into Safeway or Ralphs or to the farmers market to buy a bag of apples, which will run out in a few days—or I can apply the kingdom principle and get some apple seed to sow.

Now remember, Genesis, chapter one, verse eleven, tells us that God put the power in the seed to make itself come to pass, so there is a harvest of apples in that seed. Thus, if I apply that kingdom principle the correct way, I can get to the point when I will always have apples. I can get to the point when I will never have to go to the grocery store again for apples. I can get to the point when I will never have to spend any money again on apples. I can get to the point when I will never run out of apples.

Why? Because the harvest of apples is in the seed. God put the power in the seed to make itself come to pass. There is a whole apple tree in that apple seed. And as long as I keep planting the seeds that I get from the apples that I grow, I can end up with an orchard of apples. Why? Because God put the power in the seed to make itself come to pass.

Here, Jesus said, "When you pray, say... Hallowed be Your Name," teaching us there how to sow the Name.

Thus, just like I can sow apple seed in the natural to get apples, I can sow, or hallow, the Name of the Lord in the spiritual, to get the blessing. Why? Because the blessing is in the Name.

To illustrate, let's say I need healing in my body. I can get healing by hallowing the Name of *YHWH-Rapha*, the Lord our *Healer*.

I can say, for example, "I thank You today, O Lord my God, that You are YHWH-Rapha. You are the Lord Who heals me, and I hallow Your Name. I thank You that You were wounded for my transgressions. I give You praise, YHWH-Rapha, that You were bruised for my iniquities. I exalt You that the chastisement of My peace was laid upon You. And I give You glory, that it was by Your stripes that I am healed. You are YHWH-Rapha, You are the Lord my Healer. There is none like You. And I hallow Your holy Name."

Now, remember the kingdom principle: God put the power in the words that you speak to make themselves come to pass. Thus, as I speak the Name of the Healer, as I sow that Name in the good ground of my heart, as I embrace those words and believe those words, I am sowing seeds of healing in my body. Why? Because the healing is inside the Name. And God put the power in the Word to make itself come to pass.

Thus, Jesus is teaching us how to get the manifestation of what we seek by hallowing the Lord's Name. He is teaching us how to get the manifestation of what we seek by sowing the Lord's Name. He is teaching us how to put

#HallowingHisName

the Kingdom Principle at work. "When you pray, say: Our Father in heaven, Hallowed be Your Name." That's how you sow the Name of the Lord.

So then, to hallow the Name is to sow the Name.

And we sow the Name when we hallow the Name.

Somebody might ask, "Well, pastor, what does this business about hallowing the Name mean?" What does the word "hallow" mean? That's not something that we use in our everyday lingo.

Like many of you, I was brought up in church. And like you, we were taught to memorize what they called "The Lord Prayer," which should have been called the "Model for Prayer." And like you, we learned to say, "Our Father... Hallowed be Thy Name." However, we were never taught what that means. What does it mean to "hallow" His Name?

The Greek word is ἁγιασθήτω, which here is translated as "hallowed" and is a form of the word ἁγιάζω, which means "sanctify" or "make holy." Thus, this is something that you set apart as different. This is something that you distinguish. This is something that you treat differently from the rest. This is something that you prize and cherish.

Here, in Luke, chapter eleven, Jesus says, "*When* you pray, say, 'Hallowed be Your Name.'" Notice: He did not say, "*If* you pray." He said, "*When* you pray." Thus, there is an expectation that we are in regular communication with the Lord. He says, "When you talk to Me, say 'Hallowed be Your Name.'" He is telling us, "You need to talk to Me, and when you talk to Me, sanctify My Name."

In other words, He is telling us, "You need to talk to Me, and when you talk to Me, set My Name apart as different, distinguish My Name from any other name, make a difference between what you do with My Name and what you do with any other name, prize and cherish and celebrate and honor My Name." God expects us to talk to Him, and He admonishes us to sanctify His Name.

Hallowed be Your Name.

And this is what He means when He says to us in that twentieth chapter of Exodus, "You shall not take My Name in vain." One way that we can avoid taking the Name of the Lord our God in vain is by *hallowing* His Name.

To hallow the Name is to sow the Name.

And we sow the Name when we hallow the Name.

You sow the Name when you say, "Lord, I bless You today, that You are *YHWH-Yireh, You are the Lord my Provider.* I thank You that You provide for all of my needs, according to Your riches in glory, by Christ Jesus. I thank You, Lord, that because I bring all of my tithes into Your storehouse as You instructed, I get to prove You with it; and I get to watch You open for me the windows of heaven and pour out more blessing upon me than I have room enough to contain." And because God put the power in the Word to make itself come to pass, you are guaranteed to reap your provision.

You sow the Name when you say, "Lord, I bless You today, that You are *YHWH-Nissi, You are the Lord my Banner.* And I thank You that You fight my battles for me. And I thank You that You defend and protect me. And I thank You that You always cause me to triumph. And I thank You that You always give me victory. You cause me to be more than a conqueror, because You are YHWH-Nissi, and You are on my side."

And because God put the power in the Word to make itself come to pass, you are guaranteed to walk in victory. You cannot lose. You cannot be defeated. You will always come out on top. It's a kingdom principle. It is a spiritual law.

#HallowingHisName

You sow the Name when you say, "Lord, I glorify You today, that You are *YHWH-Rohi, You are the Lord my Shepherd.* You look out for me and feed me and satisfy me with the best of the land because You are my Shepherd. You fortify me and stimulate me and invigorate me with that which is most refreshing because You are my Shepherd. And You look after me, and sustain me, and cause me to excel and flourish in all that I do. Thank You that You are YHWH-Rohi. Thank You that You are the Lord my Shepherd."

And because God put the power in the Word to make itself come to pass, it is a done deal and a forgone conclusion that He is chasing after you. It is a done deal and a forgone conclusion that He is looking out for you. When you do this, you have sown the Word, and it cannot return void. The Word has gone out, and it must come to pass. This is a kingdom principle. It must come to pass.

You shall not take the Name of the Lord your God in vain. Sow the Name like you sow a seed. You have to talk to God. He said, "When you pray," not *if* you pray. When you *hallow* His Name, you are sowing His Name. And because God put the power in the Name to make itself come to pass, that's how you will reap your harvest.

CHAPTER 6

THE NAME AS A KINGDOM SEED

#ThePowerInTheSeedToMakeItselfComeToPass

Mark, chapter four, verses twenty-six through twenty-nine, reads as follows:

> And He said, "The kingdom of God is as if a man should scatter seed on the ground, and should sleep by night and rise by day, and the seed should sprout and grow, he himself does not know how. For the earth yields crops by itself: first the blade, then the head, after that the full grain in the head. But when the grain ripens, immediately he puts in the sickle, because the harvest has come."
>
> Mark 4:26-29

We have been referencing the power of attorney that we have been given, which entitles us to use the Name of Jesus to make requests, with the assurance that those requests will be answered because of that power of attorney.

When Jesus said, "Whatever you ask in My Name, I will do it," He was conveying to us the right to use His Name to get whatever we want. The Name of Jesus is the evidence that you possess a legal right to have or obtain "whatever it is that you ask." And it doesn't matter that the enemy does not like it, and it doesn't matter that the enemy does not want to let go, and it doesn't matter that the enemy has a stronghold on it because the Name of Jesus is your power of attorney, and the power to make it happen is in the Name.

We have also talked about using the power of attorney that you have in Jesus's Name as a tool to get what God has promised you. No matter how skilled and talented and gifted you may be, you still need your tools to get the job done.

In the last chapter, we introduced another way to look at how to avoid taking the Name of the Lord in vain. We talked about using the Name of the Lord as a seed. I want to pick up where we left off.

> And He said, "The kingdom of God is as if a man should scatter seed on the ground, and should sleep by night and rise by day, and the seed should sprout and grow, he himself does not know how […] But when the grain ripens, immediately he puts in the sickle, because the harvest has come."
>
> Mark 4:26-29

According to this passage of Scripture, the kingdom of God can be associated with seed. In other words, the sowing of seed is a kingdom principle.

God has given us the revelation that this kingdom principle of sowing seed is probably one of the most important principles that discloses how the kingdom of God operates.

Let's take a look at what Jesus said in verses thirteen and fourteen, of Mark, chapter four: "And He said to them, 'Do you not understand this parable? How then will you understand all the parables? The sower sows the Word'" (Mark 4:13-14). The explanation provided in Luke's Gospel has Jesus saying it this way: "Now the parable is this: The seed is the Word of God" (Luke 8:11).

Jesus reveals here that this kingdom principle of sowing seed is like the "granddaddy parable." He suggests very strongly that we need to get this. If you are sleepy, this is where you need to throw some water on your face. If you are distracted, this is where you need to scoot up real close and pay attention. If somebody is talking to you, this is the time that you need to ask them to hold that thought.

"Do you not understand this parable? How then will you understand all the parables?" An understanding of this parable will show you how to get your breakthrough, how to get your healing, how to get your financial miracle, how to get your prayers answered. The revelation is in this passage.

He said to them, "The sower sows the Word." And over in Luke, it says, "The seed is the Word of God."

So this is telling us that the operation of the kingdom of God can be associated with the operation of seed.

In other words, if you understand how seed operates, then you've got a picture of how the kingdom of God operates. And one of the most fascinating things about seeds is that God put within every seed the power to make itself come to pass.

Let's go to Genesis, chapter one, verse eleven, where we are introduced to the kingdom principle of seed. Here, the

#ThePowerInTheSeedToMakeItselfComeToPass

Bible says, "Then God said, 'Let the earth bring forth grass, the herb that yields seed, and the fruit tree that yields fruit according to its kind, whose seed is in itself, on the earth'; and it was so."

God put within every seed the power to make itself come to pass. That big old apple tree was on the inside of one little seed. When you take a road trip up the Interstate 5 freeway in California, you drive past the groves and groves of walnut trees. All of that came out of a single walnut, which is the seed.

When you drive through Polk County in central Florida, past the acres and acres of orchards of oranges, all of that can be traced back to a single orange seed.

But as we have discussed, it wasn't enough for those farmers just to have the seed in their possession. The kingdom principle requires that you do something with the seed: you've got to plant it. It is an indisputable fact that seeds have to be planted if you expect them to grow.

In the last chapter, I mentioned my grandmother and the packets of seed that she had stored for months and maybe even a year or more in the windowsill. As long as the seed was left in those packets in that windowsill, they remained seeds in some packets. My grandmother had to plant those seeds for them to turn into a harvest of fruits and vegetables.

And although God put within the seed the power to make itself come to pass, your part is to sow it. You've got to sow your seed if you want it to reap your harvest. "With what measure you meet it shall be measured back to you" (Mark 4:24, KJV). "Be not deceived, God is not mocked, for whatever a man sows, that is what he shall reap" (Galatians 6:7).

The revelation that we get from Mark, chapter four, which contains the "grandaddy parable," is that "the sower sows the Word." In other words, it was "the Word" that was the seed that the sower from Mark, chapter four, was sowing. So the "grandaddy parable" reveals to us that words are spiritual seeds that contain within themselves the power to make themselves come to pass. And Jesus said in Luke chapter eight, verse eleven, that "the seed is the Word of God." Thus, just like every other seed, God put within the Word the power to make itself come to pass.

Nevertheless, just like I have to sow tomato seeds if I want to see tomatoes grow, and just like I have to sow cantaloupe seeds if I want to see cantaloupe grow, I have to sow *words* if I want to see the promises of God manifest.

Why? Because God put the power in the Word to make itself come to pass. Thus, the question is, how do we sow words? How do we plant words? The way we plant our words is by speaking them.

In the last chapter, I mention that I am a big fan of apple cobbler. But what I did not mention was my love for grapes: red grapes, white grapes, black grapes, all grapes. I love grapes so much that I eat grapes 365 days per year. Generally, if you open my refrigerator, you will find an assortment of grapes. Whenever I am running low on grapes, I have some options. One is that I can go into the nearest grocery store to buy a couple of bags of grapes, knowing that those grapes will run out in a few days and I will be right where I started. Another option is that I can apply the kingdom principle and get some grape seeds to sow. This option would require me to wait longer to get the grapes in hand, but the blessing is that I would never lack grapes again.

As noted earlier, the Bible tells us in Genesis chapter one, verse eleven, that God put the power in the seed to make itself come to pass, so it follows that there is a harvest of grapes in one grape seed. If I apply that kingdom principle in the correct way, I can always have grapes and never run out. If I work this kingdom principle in the correct way, never

#ThePowerInTheSeedToMakeItselfComeToPass

again will I have to go to the grocery store for grapes. I will never have to spend any money on grapes. I will never lack grapes. This is a kingdom principle.

And it is on account of this kingdom principle that God can make as bold a declaration a He does in Malachi, chapter three, where He says in verse ten: "'Bring all the tithes into the storehouse, that there may be food in My house, and try Me now in this,' says the Lord of hosts, 'If I will not open for you the windows of heaven and pour out for you such blessing that there will not be room enough to receive it.'"

Recently, God gave me a revelation of how this works.

For this illustration, I want to switch our focus back to apples. Think about it. If you plant an apple seed in your backyard, at some point, that seed is going to grow into a tree, which is going to bring forth hundreds and hundreds of apples that will yield hundreds and hundreds of seeds. If you plant those hundreds and hundreds of seeds in your backyard, they are going to yield hundreds and hundreds of trees, each of which will bring forth hundreds and hundreds of apples, which will yield hundreds and hundreds of seeds. At some point, as this cycle continues, you will run out of room in your backyard and will not have room for any more trees.

Why? Because the harvest of apples is in the seed. God put the power in the seed to make itself come to pass. There is a whole apple tree in one little apple seed. And as long as I keep planting the seed that I get from the apples that I grow, I can end up with an orchard of apples. Why? Because God put the power in the seed to make itself come to pass.

When Jesus said, "When you pray, say... Hallowed be Your Name," He was teaching us how to sow the Name as a spiritual seed.

Just like I can sow apple seed in the natural to get apples, I can sow, or hallow, the Name of the Lord in the spiritual to

DR. MELVIN G. BARNEY, ESQ.

get the blessing. Why? Because the blessing is in the Name. And with whatever measure you meet, it shall be measured to you. If you don't plant the seeds, you won't grow the corn.

Likewise, if you don't hallow the Name, or if you don't sow the Name, that might be what's keeping you from getting your body healed.

Just like I can keep running back to Safeway and Ralphs and the farmers market every time I run of apples, you can keep running back to the doctor for a shot of cortisone whenever "old Arthur" kicks up. Or just like I can get some apple seed and sow it in my backyard to guarantee that I never run out of apples, you can keep on sowing your spiritual seed by personalizing the promises, saying such things as:

> "Lord, I thank you that you are my YHWH-Rapha. You are the God Who heals me.

> "In Your Word, you said, 'If [I] diligently hearken to the voice of the Lord [my] God, and wilt do that which is right in [Your] sight, and wilt give ear to [Your] commandments, and keep all [Your] statutes, [You] will put none of these diseases upon [me], which [You] brought upon the Egyptians: for [You are] the Lord that heals [me]' [see Exodus 15:26].

> "And You said for me to 'Bless the Lord, O my soul, and forget not all [Your] benefits: [because You] forgive all [my] iniquities; [and You] heal all [my] diseases' [see Psalm 103:2-3].

#ThePowerInTheSeedToMakeItselfComeToPass

"And I thank You, Lord, that [You] 'sent [Your] Word, and healed [me], and delivered [me] from [my] destructions'" [see Psalm 107:20].

"So in accordance with Your instructions, I 'attend to [Your] Words; [and I] incline [my] ear unto [Your] sayings. [And I do not let] them not depart from [my] eyes; [but I] keep them in the midst of [my] heart. For they are life unto [me because I have found] them, and health to all [my] flesh" [see Proverbs 4:20-22].

"For 'Surely [You] have borne our griefs and carried our sorrows: [even though they] esteemed [You] stricken, smitten of God, and afflicted. But [You were] wounded for [my] transgression, [You were] bruised for [my] iniquities: the chastisement of [my] peace was upon [You]; and with [Your] stripes [I am] healed' [See Isaiah 53:4-5]."

And because God put the power in the Word to make itself come to pass, you are guaranteed to see your body healed. Those dry bones will regain their strength. Why? Because God's Word cannot return to Him void. It's a kingdom principle. It is a spiritual law.

But if you won't hallow the Name, or if you won't sow the Name, that might be what's keeping you from getting your finances in order.

Just like I can keep running back to Safeway and Ralphs and the farmers market every time I run of apples, you can keep trying to figure out how "to rob Peter to pay Paul." "If I juggle this around, I can do that." And "if I just move this over here, that will get me through that." Or, just like I can get some apple seed and sow it in my backyard to guarantee that I never run out of apples, you can keep on sowing your seed, which is your tithes and offerings, and get a hold of His Name, saying things like:

> "Lord, I thank you, that you are My YHWH-Yireh. You are the God Who meets all my needs according to Your riches in glory by Christ Jesus.

> "You promised in Your Word that 'This book of the law shall not depart out of [my] mouth; but [I am to] meditate therein day and night, that [I] may observe to do according to all that is written therein: for then [You said, I] will make [my] way prosperous, and then [I] will have good success' [see Joshua 1:8].

> "You also instructed me to 'remember [You,] the Lord [my] God: for it is [You] Who gives [me] power to get wealth, that [You] may establish [Your] covenant which [You] swore to [my] fathers, as it is this day' [see Deuteronomy 8:18].

> "And then, God, You gave me a promised that if I 'Honor [You] with [my]

#ThePowerInTheSeedToMakeItselfComeToPass

67

substance, and with the first fruits of all [my] increase: [You said] so would [my] barns be filled with plenty, and [my] presses would burst out with new wine' [Proverbs 3:9-10].

"You also said, 'If [I am] willing and obedient, [I will] eat the good of the land' [see Isaiah 1:19].

"But Lord, You also instructed me to 'Bring all the tithes into the storehouse, that there may be meat in [Your] house, and prove [You] with it, [that You would] open you the windows of heaven, and pour [me] out a blessing, that there shall not be room enough to receive it' [see Malachi 3:10]."

And because God put the power in the Word to make itself come to pass, you are guaranteed to come out on top. You will always abound and have more than enough. It is a kingdom principle. It is a spiritual law.

The Bible says, "You shall not take the Name of the Lord your God in vain." You've got to sow the Name like you sow a seed.

When you hallow His Name, bless His Name, glorify His Name, you are sowing His Name. And when you sow the Name, you will reap your harvest. It is a kingdom principle that must come to pass because God put the power in the Word to make itself come to pass, and God put the power in the Name to make itself come to pass.

DR. MELVIN G. BARNEY, ESQ.

CHAPTER 7

ELOHIYM—GOD THE CREATOR

#UseYourWords

Our foundation scripture comes from Exodus, chapter twenty, in verse seven: "You shall not take the Name of the LORD your God in vain, for the LORD will not hold him guiltless who takes His Name in vain" (Exodus 20:7).

For the remaining chapters, we will add a second foundation scripture, an admonition from the Lord Jesus, Himself, found in the eleventh chapter of St. Luke, in verse two, which reads: "He said to them, 'When you pray, say: Our Father in heaven, Hallowed be Your Name'" (Luke 11:2).

We have been talking a lot about the fact that God commands us not to take or carry or bear His Name in vain. He wants us to recognize the power of attorney that we have in His Name. In speaking directly to us, the Lord Himself said, "If you ask *anything* in My Name, I will do it." You have the power of attorney to act on behalf of the Most High God.

We have also made a note of the fact that God wants us to see His Name as a tool that we need to use to gain possession of the blessing, in the same way that a carpenter would use a hammer and a saw to build a set of kitchen cabinets.

We have also discovered that God wants us to learn how to see His Name as a seed that we've got to sow in order to cause the promises of the Word to manifest. A farmer who plants apple seed in a field in order to get apple trees knows that as long as he sows his seed, he will get some apple trees that will produce more seeds that will yield more apple trees. And he knows that he can end up with an apple orchard as long as he continues to sow.

Why? Because the harvest of apples is in the seed, and God put the power in the seed to make itself come to pass. There is a whole apple tree inside that little apple seed. And as long as I keep planting the seeds that I get from the apples that I grow, I can end up with an orchard of apples. Because God put the power in the seed to make itself come to pass.

Here, when Jesus instructs us in prayer to say, "Hallowed be Your Name," He is teaching us how to sow the Name.

To hallow the Name is to sow the Name.

And to sow the Name is to hallow the Name.

So just like I can sow apple seed in the natural to get apples, I can sow, or hallow, the Name of the Lord in the spiritual, to get the blessing of the Name. Why? Because the blessing is in the Name.

If I want a guarantee that I will get the manifestation of what the Name promises, I've got to sow the Name. And the way I sow the Name is to say the Name. That's the kingdom of God.

Now let's head back over to Genesis, chapter one. When we talk about sowing the Name, and speaking the Name, and the fact that God put the power in the seed to make itself come to pass, this is where we get the explanation as to how the kingdom of God operates.

In Genesis, chapter one, at verse one, the Scripture says: "In the beginning God [*Elohiym*] created the heavens and the earth."

Let me pause for a moment and point out parenthetically that the Hebrew word that is translated "God" in this passage of Scripture is *Elohiym*, which literally means "the Gods." This speaks to the Trinity: God the Father, God the Word or Son, and God the Holy Spirit.

But as we can see right here in verse one, this "in-the-beginning God," also known as Elohiym, is identified as the Creator. And the revelation that we get about Him from this first book of the Bible is that He creates things by using His Words.

I have often watched when a mother is dealing with a whining child who wants something, but instead of asking, he will whine and cry and throw a fit. Sometimes that mother, with the patience that only a mother can have, will say, "Use your words." And this is the word of the Lord to the saints today. If you want something, don't whine. Don't throw a hissy fit. Don't murmur and complain. Just open up your mouth and use your words.

Now let's go back into this text and pick up where we were; and if we substitute the Hebrew into this passage of Scripture in the places where it has been translated "God," it would read as follows:

> In the beginning Elohiym created the heavens and the earth. The earth was without form, and void; and darkness was on the face of the deep. And the Spirit of Elohiym was hovering over the face of the waters. Then Elohiym said, "Let there be light"; and there was light.
> Genesis 1:1-3, modified

#UseYourWords

A little further down in this passage, the Scripture reads:

> Then Elohiym said, "Let the earth bring
> forth grass, the herb that yields seed, and
> the fruit tree that yields fruit according
> to its kind, whose seed is in itself, on the
> earth"; and it was so [...] Then Elohiym
> said, "Let Us make man in Our image,
> according to Our likeness; let them have
> dominion over the fish of the sea, over
> the birds of the air, and over the cattle,
> over all the earth and over every creeping
> thing that creeps on the earth."
>
> Genesis 1:11, 26, modified

And then verse twenty-seven says: "So Elohiym created man in His own image; in the image of Elohiym He created him; male and female Elohiym created them" (Genesis 1:27, modified).

Right off the top, there are three things about Elohiym that I want us to grab ahold of from Genesis, chapter one.

The first is this: Genesis, chapter one, is where we get our introduction to God. We are introduced to Elohiym, the Most High God, in Genesis, chapter one. We learn of His trinitarian nature in Genesis, chapter one, as He says, "Let us," speaking to the other members of the Godhead. We learn that He is eternal in Genesis, chapter one, from digging in deeper and finding that He existed as God even before this "in the beginning" was. We learn that He is amazing and all-powerful in Genesis, chapter one, as we see Him cause everything that exists to sprout into existence from nothing. And we learn in Genesis, chapter one, that Elohiym is a talking God. Elohiym likes to talk. Genesis, chapter one, is where we get our introduction to the talking God.

In verse one, we see that after God took note of the fact that the state and condition of things were contrary to His will, God started talking. The earth was without form and void. It was chaotic. Not God's will. Darkness was all over the face of the deep. It was lifeless. Not God's will.

Because the state and condition of things were contrary to God's will, He started talking. It was as if He said, "This darkness is not My will: light be... I don't want this chaos. Earth come forth, and dry land appear... I don't want it lifeless. Grass and herbs and trees and plants, I want you to sprout up."

God started talking about everything He wanted. Now notice, He *did not talk* about what He *did not want*. He *called forth* what He *did want*. Point one is that God is a talking God Who likes to talk.

The second point that I want us to extract from Genesis, chapter one, about God is that Elohiym uses Words to create things and that Elohiym uses Words to change things. Elohiym has so much confidence in His Word that He says "it was so" *before* it manifests and *before* it actually is so!

Verse eleven says, "Then Elohiym said, 'Let the earth bring forth grass, the herb that yields seed, and the fruit tree that yields fruit according to its kind, whose seed is in itself, on the earth'; and it was so" (Genesis 1:11).

Before a blade of grass had grown, God said it *was* so. Notice this: He did not say, "It *will be* so." He said, "It *was* so." As far as God is concerned, once He says it, it is a done deal. You can go on about your business because He is done with it, and it has no choice but to come to pass. Once God says it, you can take it to the bank. Once He says it, it is a forgone conclusion.

#UseYourWords

God uses Words to create things, and God uses Words to change things. God has so much confidence in His Word that He says that it was so, even before it actually is so.

And when you think about it, isn't that what He did with us? Before we were righteous, He reckoned us as righteous, deemed us worthy, called us cleansed, and sanctified us—when we were yet wallowing in our sins and in our mess.

Okay. I feel a "preaching moment" coming up now. You might be able to sit there today and look all holy and prissy and important if you want to, but if we were to rewind the video and take a glimpse back down memory lane from where you came... Hallelujah! You know what the Lord brought you out of. You know what God delivered you from. You know what God did for you when there was no way and when there was no hope. Somebody said it this way: "He brought me out of darkness into His marvelous light"; "He brought me from a mighty long way." Every once in a while, when I think about what great things the Lord has done, I feel a "preaching moment" coming on. But I have to remember I am writing a book, not preaching a sermon!

God uses Words to create things, and God uses Words to change things. And God has so much confidence in His Word that He says that it was so, and He says that it is good, even before there is any sign of the "is so-ness" or any sign of the "is good-ness."

Thus, the second point that we can get about God out of Genesis, chapter one, is that Elohiym uses Words to create things and Elohiym uses Words to change things.

Point number three. In Genesis, chapter one, in verse twenty-six, Elohiym said, "Let Us make man in Our image, according to Our likeness."

Up to now, in Genesis, chapter one, we see God use Words to create heaven and earth. We see God use Words to create day and night. We see God use Words to create seasons and time. We see the Lord use Words to create vegetation, and birds, and fish, and what Ellie Mae Clampett from *The Beverly Hillbillies* called "critters." And with respect to all of the living things that God created, we also see the kingdom principle at work because when He created them, God also spoke in them the ability to reproduce after their own kind. In other words, Elohiym put within everything that lives, plant and animal, the power to make itself come to pass.

But as we get down to verse twenty-six, we see that God veered off track a little when He got to mankind. It says in verse twenty-six, "Then Elohiym said, 'Let Us make man in *Our* image, according to *Our* likeness'" (Genesis 1:26, emphasis added). So God spoke in us, mankind, the ability to produce after *His* own kind. That's the kingdom principle at its best.

The Bible says that when it came to us, God said, "Let Us make man in *Our* image, and let Us make man after *Our* likeness." God spoke into us the ability to produce after God's own kind.

He created us in His own image, meaning we are a reflection of God. This speaks of our authority on the earth. We were created to do what God does. We were created to mirror God. We were created to reflect God. What is it to reflect God?

To reflect God is to look like God looks. To reflect God is to operate in authority. To reflect God is to operate in dominion. To reflect God is to operate in responsibility. So, we reflect God by creating whatever God wants to be created. We reflect God by changing whatever God wants changed. We are to operate in the image of God.

Additionally, the Bible says that Elohiym went on to say, "Let Us create man after Our likeness." Well, what does

#UseYourWords

that mean? It means God has given us the ability to act like Him. He has given us the ability to imitate Him.

We learn from Genesis, chapter one, that God uses Words to create things that are according to His will and that God uses Words to change things that are out of alignment with His will. From this, we can take note that the way we are to imitate God is by using our words to create things that are in accordance with God's will and by using our words to change things that are out of alignment with His will.

Just like God used Words to create things that are according to His Will, we have been given an assignment, which is to use our words to create whatever things that are according to God's will. And just like God uses Words to change things that are out of alignment with His will, we have been given an assignment, which is to use our words to change whatever things that are out of alignment with His will.

"Well," somebody might ask, "how do we do that?" We do it as God did it. Just like God, we've got to call those things that "be not as though they were" (Romans 4:17, KJV). And arguably, the best biblical reference we have to illustrate this principle is found in Genesis, chapter seventeen, when God changed Abram's name to Abraham.

God said, "I told you twenty-four years ago that I was going to give you a child. And you have been floundering around with the promise. And you have been fumbling around with the promise. And you have been sometimes up. And you have been sometimes down. So, let me go ahead and show you how to do this. You've got to sow your spiritual seed. You've got to speak this thing. You've got to use your words."

Then God said, "Your name shall no longer be called Abram, but Abraham, for a father of many nations have I made you. So you've got to speak this thing into existence. You've got to operate in My image. You've got to act according to My likeness. You've got to reflect Elohiym. You've got to act like Elohiym. You've got to create what needs to be created with your words. You've got to change what needs to be changed with your words. You've got to use your words."

Now all of a sudden, Abraham is speaking it and sowing his spiritual seed. Now all of a sudden, out of his mouth, he is calling himself a father of many nations. He's sowing his spiritual seed. And the next thing they knew, Sarah was pregnant. And the next thing they knew, Sarah gave birth. And the next thing they knew, Sarah was rocking a baby in her arms. And the next thing they knew, Sarah was laughing, and Abraham was laughing, and God was laughing! How is that so? Because God put the power in the words to make themselves come to pass. That's the kingdom of God!

Just like Abraham, you have got to embrace the fact that Elohiym is a talking God. You have to embrace the fact that Elohiym uses words to create things that need to be created. You have to embrace the fact that Elohiym uses words to change things that need to be changed. And you have to embrace the fact that you were created in His image and according to His likeness.

Moreover, you have to embrace the fact that you must use your words to create the things that you want to see come to pass in your life. And you have to embrace the fact that you must use your words to change the obstacles that you want to see moved out of your way.

God put the power in the seed to make itself come to pass. That's the kingdom of God. Elohiym sows His spiritual seed by speaking. You also sow your spiritual seed by speaking. You are created in God's image. You are created after God's likeness. When you open up your mouth and speak,

#UseYourWords

you are sowing your spiritual seed. When you hallow His Name, you sow His Name. And the way you sow His Name is by speaking His Name.

So, instead of using your words to talk about how bad it has gotten and how horrible things are, you need to use your words to talk about the victory you have in Christ Jesus.

And instead of using your words to talk about how the devil is chasing you and how he has been on your back all week long, you need to use your words to talk about the authority you have over him and the fact that he is under your feet.

And instead of using your words to talk about how much pain you feel and every negative thing the doctor said to you, you need to use your words to talk about how He was wounded for your transgressions, was bruised for your iniquities, and how it is by His stripes that you are healed.

And instead of using your words to talk about how bad the economy is and that you don't know how you are going to make it, you need to use your words to talk about the fact that your God shall supply all your need and how He has made you the head and not the tail.

And instead of using your words to talk about all of the trouble your children are getting into, you need to use your words to talk about the fact that your children are taught of the Lord, and great shall be their peace.

You are created in the image of Elohiym. You are created after the likeness of Elohiym. Elohiym is a talking God. Elohiym uses words to create the things He wants. Elohiym uses words to change the things He does not want. You have been authorized to use your words to create what is in accordance with the will of God. You have been authorized to use your words to change whatever is out of alignment with the will of God. God has instructed us to call those things "which be not as though they were." Use your words. It is with the same "measure you mete, [that] it shall be measured unto you again" (Mark 4:24, KJV).

CHAPTER 8

EL SHADDAI—THE ALMIGHTY GOD

#JustLikeAMother

The foundation scriptures for this teaching come from Exodus, chapter twenty, and Luke, chapter eleven, which read, respectively, as follows:

> "You shall not take the Name of the LORD your God in vain, for the LORD will not hold him guiltless who takes His Name in vain" (Exodus 20:7).

> "He said to them, 'When you pray, say: Our Father in heaven, Hallowed be Your Name'" (Luke 11:2).

In the last chapter, we were introduced to Elohiym, the talking God. We found Him to be a God Who likes to talk. The Scripture says, "In the beginning God created the heavens and the earth." And as we plowed our way through that first chapter of the Bible, where we get our first encounter with God, the Creator, we found that the way God created everything that He created…was by talking.

Over in Hebrews chapter eleven, the Scripture says in verse three, "By faith we understand that the worlds were framed by the word of God, so that the things which are seen were not made of things which are visible" (Hebrews 11:3).

In other words, if you were to investigate God's method of creating all that He created, you would not find a hammer or any nails on the scene in Genesis, chapter one. Here, where I am in downtown Los Angeles, at the time of this writing, they are constructing a bunch of skyscrapers, so there are cranes all over the place. But God did not make use of a crane when He constructed the Rocky Mountains.

Some friends of mine recently had a pool installed in their backyard, and after they obtained permission from their neighbors to temporarily move the neighbor's fencing, my friends had to hire a contractor to bring in the necessary digging equipment. But God did not hire a crew to dig out the Pacific Ocean.

What did God do? God started talking. God talked this thing into existence. The Bible says, "By faith we understand that the worlds were framed *by the Word of God!*" He says the things that you see were not made of tangible things: everything that was made was made by God's Words. We serve a God Who talks. He calls forth the things that He wants, and while He is talking, He acts as though the things he is talking about already exist!

In Chapter 7, we said it this way: Elohiym has so much confidence in His Word that He says "it was so" even *before* it actually is so. Why is that? Because God put the power in the Word to make itself come to pass. So when God speaks, you'd better get ready.

DR. MELVIN G. BARNEY, ESQ.

When God started talking to Noah about a flood, they didn't even know what rain was… They had never seen rain before.

The Bible says, up to that point, the earth watered itself by a mist that would come up out of the ground. Think of that sprinkler system that you paid all of that money to have installed in your yard. That was not a contemporary invention. They got that idea from God! Back in Noah's day, they had never heard of rain, so when God started talking about rain, the people didn't believe Him.

When Noah got ahold of the Word, he embraced it and started preaching that it was going to rain. But even then, the people laughed him to scorn. All the while Noah was out there building the ark, they were laughing at him, and mocking him, and making fun of him…until the day the deluge hit, and it all broke open. God put the power in the Word to make itself come to pass.

When God started talking to Abraham about having a child, he was already seventy-five years old, and the Bible says his body was "as good as dead." And after about ten years of waiting, Abraham said, "Lord, You keep talking to me about all of this stuff you are going to do for my descendants and me, but what are you going to give me seeing I go childless? Do I need to remind you that I do not have a single child, and this Eliezer of Damascus who works for me is my heir?" (see Genesis 15:1-3).

When God talks, you had better get ready. Why? Because God put the power in the Word to make itself come to pass.

In response, God said, "He shall not be your heir, for one who comes out of your own bowels shall be your heir." God said, "Look up at those stars in the sky and start counting." He said, "So shall your seed be" (see Genesis 15:4-5)

#JustLikeAMother

as if to say, "you need to go home, grab Sarah, put on some Teddy Pendergrass, and handle your business," because it is impossible for God to lie.

When God talks, you had better get ready. Why? Because God put the power in the Word to make itself come to pass.

In the last chapter when we studied Elohiym, there were three takeaways about Elohiym that I want to make sure we internalize.

1. Elohiym is a talking God. He likes to talk. God started talking in Genesis, chapter one. God kept on talking up through Revelation, chapter twenty. And God is still talking to those who will hear His voice today. Elohiym is a talking God.

2. Elohiym uses Words to create things, and Elohiym uses Words to change things. Everything that God creates, He creates with Word. God uses Words to cause His very will to come into existence. And if something is out of alignment with His will, God uses Words to change it.

3. Elohiym created us in His image and after His likeness. We are to reflect Him. We are to act like Him. We have been commissioned to use our words to create that which is in accordance with God's will, and we have been commissioned to use our words to change those things that are out of alignment with God's will.

Now let's go to Genesis, chapter seventeen, and begin reading from verse one:

> When Abram was ninety-nine years old,
> the Lord appeared to Abram and said to

him, "I am Almighty God [*El Shaddai*];
walk before Me and be blameless [a man
of integrity]. And I will make [work] My
covenant between Me and you, and will
multiply you exceedingly."

Genesis 17:1-2, modified

What is translated as "Almighty God" here comes
from the Hebrew *El Shaddai*. God said to Abram, "I am El
Shaddai."

Now keep in mind, Abram was originally from Padan-
Aran, which was a pagan, idolatrous nation that worshiped
idols as their gods. Idolatry was all Abram knew when, at the
age of seventy-five, God chose him and told him to "get up
out of [his] country and away from [his] kindred and out of
[his] father's house, and go to a land that [God] will show
[him]" (see Genesis 12:1-3).

When Abram was told to do that, he did not know anything about God's integrity. He did not know anything about
God's faithfulness. He did not know anything about God's
omnipotence. He did not know anything about God. All he
knew was that there is something different about *this* God
because *this* God talks. Abram might have thought, *Of all
of those idols that we are accustomed to worshipping in Padan-
Aram, I have never had one talk to me. I have never had one
challenge me. I have never had one promise me a miracle.*

*There is something different about this God, and here He
is talking to me about having kids when Sarai and I have struggled during the course of our entire marriage to get pregnant? We
resigned a long, long time ago that it was not going to happen.
We gave up hope on that twenty, maybe thirty years ago. We
have already settled in on, and given up on, and resigned on,*

#JustLikeAMother

85

and coped with the que sera, sera (that is, the "whatever will be, will be").

Abram said, "We let that go a long time ago and figured it would just be Sarai and me all by ourselves."

But God has a way of re-awakening in you some of the things that you let go of a long time ago. God has a way of stirring up on the inside of you some of the things that you resigned a long time ago would never happen. God has a way of turning you around and setting you back on track and causing you to think that maybe the *que-sera-seras* do not have to be the "whatever-will-be-will-bes."

And so when we come back over here to our text, in Genesis, chapter seventeen, the Scripture says that Abraham was ninety-nine years old. By this time, God had changed his name from Abram to Abraham, God had changed Sarah's name from Sarai to Sarah, and twenty-four years have elapsed since God made the promise. But no doubt that in the midst of his struggle with this, Abraham was thinking, *Now God has been good to me over these twenty-four years. He has blessed me abundantly and increased me mightily. He has made me wealthy, and fought my battles for me, and caused my name to be great. So maybe I should just be okay with that. Maybe it doesn't matter if He doesn't do the rest. Perhaps I should just be okay with the fact that God has done what He has done.*

But the Bible says it is not so. The Bible says that God showed up when Abraham was ninety-nine years old and said, "I am El Shaddai—I am the Almighty God—if you just walk before Me and be [a man of integrity], I will complete exactly what I said I would do" (see Genesis 17:1-2). God is a finisher. God is a completer.

When God gives you a promise, you don't have to analyze it. You don't have to re-write it. You don't have to make excuses for it. You don't have to settle for less. God said, "I am El Shaddai, you just do *your* part, which is to walk in faith and integrity. That's *your* lane. You do *your* part and stay in *your* land, and *I* will do *My* part and stay in *My* lane because I've got Mine." God is a finisher. God is a completer.

Saints, we really need to learn how to focus on our part and let God do His part. He said your part is to walk in faith and integrity. And if we would just stay focused on that, it would keep us occupied until we get the breakthrough.

But because we get so focused on God's part, and whether He is going to do what He said, and why do I have to wait so long, and maybe there is something I can do to move this along—that's where we get in trouble. When we lose sight of our part and try to work out God's part, we get discouraged, because there is no way we can do God's part.

Here, after God allowed Abraham and Sarah to have their pity parties, and waiver back and forth, and focus on the fact that they were too old and that Sarah was barren, and plot to let Hagar (the concubine) act as a surrogate, and laugh back and forth at God in unbelief, and get discouraged, and lose hope—after all of that, God said, "I am going to do what I said I would do. It might appear hopeless to you, but I am El Shaddai, I am the Almighty God, is there anything too hard for the Lord?

"I don't care if you are ninety-nine, and it does not matter to Me that Sarah is eighty-nine and barren; at the appointed time, I will return to do just what I said. I am El Shaddai. I am the Almighty God.

"It does not concern Me that you are tired, and it does not matter to Me that you just want to be done; at the appointed time, I will return to do just what I said. I am El Shaddai. I am the Almighty God.

"It doesn't matter to Me that you've lost hope, and it does not matter to Me that you think you don't want it any

#JustLikeAMother

longer; at the appointed time, I will return to do just what I said. I am El Shaddai. I am the Almighty God.

"I am going to do what I said I would do. Is there anything too hard for the Lord? (see Genesis 18:14). I am El Shaddai."

While we are here, let's just dissect this revelation of El Shaddai from the Hebrew and see what it means.

El Shaddai is translated in many of our English Bibles as "God Almighty" or "the Almighty God." But let's take it apart bit by bit in Hebrew.

El in Hebrew means "God." *El* is God in its singular form. Remember in the last chapter, we looked at *Elohiym* and learned that *Elohiym* is God in its plural form. Thus, when the Bible tells us, "in the beginning, Elohiym created the heavens and the earth," it is literally saying, "in the beginning Gods [plural], created the heavens and the earth."

So *Elohiym* is speaking of the trinity. *Elohiym* is referring to the Godhead at work, God the Father, God the Word or Son, and God the Holy Spirit working together as One, creating the heavens and the earth.

Here, *El* is the singular form of God, but it is still referring to God. This is not a different God. It is still God, but it is God in His singular form. That's *El*. So *El* = God.

Now let's take a look at *Shaddai*. To further dissect the meaning of *Shaddai*, let's break it up into syllables.

The Hebrew *shad* means "breast," which in this context would mean the "Breasted One." Well, what is a breast? A breast is the source of nourishment.

The first thing a newborn baby craves after entering into this new world is his mother's breast milk.

After the struggle and trauma he had to endure to get down that birth canal, and after being slapped on the bottom by the doctor who delivered him, and after having to look in the face of all these nurses who are grinning at him, he just wants them to hand him over to momma because all he wants right now is momma's breast milk. That baby somehow knows instinctively that his mother's breast is the source of his nourishment.

So here, *Shad*, which translates as "Breast," is referring to the Breasted One, signifying the One Who nourishes. When we talk about *Shad*, it signifies the One Who supplies. When we talk about *Shad*, it signifies the One Who satisfies. He is our Source.

And now, let's look at the Hebrew *dai*. The *dai* refers to One Who sheds forth. The *dai* is defined as One Who pours out. The *dai* speaks to One Who heaps benefits.

Someone may ask, "What is all of this talking about?" This is talking about *provision*. This is talking about *sustenance*. This is talking about *abundance*. This is talking about *blessing*.

It paints an image of somebody coming up to you who just continues to dole out to you more abundance than you can handle. It paints an image of a dump truck pulling up to your house and heaping loads and loads of blessing upon you that you can't even contain. It paints an image of the windows of heaven being opened up for you and pouring out more blessings on you than you have the room to receive.

Thus, when we examine the *dai*, we are talking about the One Who has no limits. When we talk about the *dai*, we are talking about the One Who is all bountiful.

When God reveals Himself to Abraham as El Shaddai, He is saying, "I am your Source, and I am about to load you up with an increase." When God reveals Himself to Abraham as El Shaddai, He is saying, "I am your All-Powerful Nourisher, and I am about to heap bountiful blessings upon you." And when

#JustLikeAMother

God reveals Himself to Abraham as El Shaddai, He is saying, "I am the Almighty God, and I am about to blow you up."

And this talking God, Who likes to talk, is saying the same thing to you today. He is *El Shaddai*, which means "the Almighty God." *El Shaddai* means "The Source." *El Shaddai* means "The Nourisher." *El Shaddai* means "The Breasted One." *El Shaddai* means "The Nurse." *El Shaddai* means "The All-Sufficient One." And *El Shaddai* means "the God *Who is More Than Enough*." He is *El Shaddai*. He is the Almighty God.

You might say, "But I am too old now, and it's just too late." But God is saying, "I am El Shaddai, and there is nothing too hard for the Lord."

You might say, "But it's too messed up now, and everything has come apart at the seams." But God is saying, "I am El Shaddai, and there is nothing too hard for the Lord."

You might say, "But the doctor told me the condition is incurable. The doctor said the condition is irreversible." But God is saying, "I am El Shaddai, and there is nothing too hard for the Lord."

He is El Shaddai.

What do you have to do if you need El Shaddai to manifest in your situation? Jesus said you've got to hallow His Name. What do you need to do if you want El Shaddai to take on your circumstance? You've got to sow your spiritual seed. Why? Because God put the power in the seed to make itself come to pass. And the title of El Shaddai is a seed that contains within itself the power to make itself come to pass.

Well, how do you sow seed in the natural? You've got to plant it.

And how do you sow seed in the spiritual? You've got to speak it.

Just like you have to plant apple seeds if you want a harvest of apples, you have to plant the title of the El Shaddai if you want the Almighty God to be at work on your behalf. Why? Because God put the power in the word to make itself come to pass. And the more you plant, the more you get. Why? Because it is with the same "measure you mete, it shall be measured unto you."

Jesus said, "After this manner pray, say, 'Hallowed be Your Name.'" If we want the manifestation of what the Name entails, we've got to hallow the Name. If we want the manifestation of what the Name promises, we have to hallow the Name.

Therefore, instead of talking about how hard it is and how you don't know if you can make it, you've got to sow the Name. "I thank You, oh God, that You are El Shaddai, You are the Almighty God, and there is nothing too hard for You."

And instead of saying, "Well, I am just too old now, and it is just too late now," you've got to sow the Name. "I thank You, oh God, that You are El Shaddai, you are my Source. You give power to the feeble, and to those who have no might, you increase strength."

And instead of saying, "But it's too messed up now, and everything has come apart at the seams," you've got to sow the Name. "I thank You, oh God, that You are El Shaddai, you are the All-Sufficient One, and you work all things together for good to those of us who love You and who are the called according to Your purpose."

And instead of saying, "I just don't know how I'm going to get my bills paid. I just don't know how I'm going to make it," you've got to sow the Name. "I thank You, oh God, that You are El Shaddai, you are the God *Who is More Than*

#JustLikeAMother

Enough, and you supply all of my need, according to Your riches in glory by Christ Jesus."

And instead of saying, "But the doctor told me to get my house in order because I only have three months to live," you've got to sow the Name. "I thank You, oh God, that You are El Shaddai. You are my Nourisher, my Sustenance, my Way-Maker, my Nurse, and my Healer; and you were wounded for my transgressions, and You were bruised for my iniquities, and by Your stripes, I am healed."

He is El Shaddai. He is your Source. Your Nurse. Your Nourisher. The Breasted One. The God *Who is More Than Enough.*

CHAPTER 9

YHWH—THE PERSONAL NAME OF GOD

#AWhole'NotherLevel

Let's head over to the sixth chapter of the book of Exodus, where we will read verses two and three.

> And God [Elohiym] spoke to Moses and said to him: "I am [YHWH]. I appeared to Abraham, to Isaac, and to Jacob, as [El Shaddai], but by My Name [YHWH] I was not known to them."
>
> Exodus 6:2-3, modified

I also want to revisit the foundation scriptures that we have adopted for this teaching, which come, respectively, from Exodus, chapter twenty, and Luke, chapter eleven.

> "You shall not take the Name of the LORD your God in vain, for the LORD

will not hold him guiltless who takes His Name in vain" (Exodus 20:7).

"He said to them, 'When you pray, say: Our Father in heaven, Hallowed be Your Name'" (Luke 11:2).

We have been learning how these passages of Scripture relate to the kingdom principle of sowing and reaping. For Jesus Himself said, "The kingdom of God is as if a man should scatter seed on the ground" (Mark 4:26).

The Holy Spirit has given us the revelation that to hallow the Name is to sow the Name and to sow the Name is to hallow the Name. And in case somebody wants to know how to sow the Name? You sow the Name by speaking the Name.

You sow the Name by thanking God that He is Who He says He is. You sow the Name by saying, "I thank You, Lord, for being for me, Who You say You Are." And because God put the power in the seed to make itself come to pass, just like in the natural, when you plant some lettuce seeds in your backyard, as long as you toil the ground and water it, and protect that seed from bugs, in due season, you will have lettuce. Likewise, when you sow the Name, and keep speaking it, and stay positive, and walk by faith, and operate in obedience, it shall come to pass. Why? Because God put the power in the Word to make itself come to pass.

In Chapter 7, we were introduced to Elohiym, the talking God. We found Him to be a God Who likes to talk. We were able to glean from Genesis, chapter one, that Elohiym created everything that He created by talking. He calls forth the things that He wants, and while He is talking, He acts as though the things He is talking about already exist!

When Elohiym speaks, it is a done deal, and as a matter of fact, He has so much confidence in His Word that He says "it was so" even before it actually is so. Why is that? Because God put the power in the Word to make itself come to pass.

Then in Chapter 8, we got into the revelation of God as El Shaddai, the Almighty God. In dissecting *El Shaddai* in Hebrew, we discover that there is nobody greater. El Shaddai is the Self-Contained, All-Abundant One. He is the One Who contains within Himself everything that we need to abound and flourish. God does not need anything outside of Himself to attend to us. God does not need anything outside of Himself to look after us. God does not need anything outside of Himself to take care of us.

El Shaddai is the One Who supplies. He is the One Who satisfies. He is "the God *Who is More Than Enough.*" El Shaddai means He is not a God of lack. That's not Him. He is not a God of "just enough." That's not Him. The Scripture describes Him as the One Who does "exceedingly, abundantly above all that we ask or think" (see Ephesians 3:20). That's El Shaddai. Our God, El Shaddai, is the God *Who is More Than Enough.*

As amazing and powerful and overwhelming a revelation of Who Elohiym is and what Elohiym means, and Who El Shaddai is and what El Shaddai means, when we go over to Exodus, chapter six, God takes us further into the revelation of Who He is. Beginning from verse two, the Scripture says: "And *Elohiym* spoke to Moses and said to him: 'I am *YHWH.* I appeared to Abraham, to Isaac, and to Jacob, as *El Shaddai,* but by My Name *YHWH* I was not known to them.'"

"Abraham and Isaac and Jacob knew Me by My title, Elohiym, but I never told either of them My Name. They did not get to know My Name.

"Abraham and Isaac and Jacob knew Me by My title, El Shaddai, but I never told either of them My Name. They did not get to know My Name.

"The time has come for Me to reveal to you what I did not disclose to them. I no longer want you to know of Me only by title: now I want you to know Me by My Name. So let Me introduce Myself: I am *YHWH*." And with the revelation of His *Name*, God was taking it to "a whole 'nother level."

Let's pause here for a moment and talk about the difference between a person's *title* and that person's *name*.

Your *title* describes what you do. It provides people with information about you. It gives people a synopsis of what they can expect from you.

To illustrate, let's say you are a high school principal. High school principal is your title. That title, high school principal, tells us what you do. We know from your title that you are the principal assigned to a high school. We know from your title that you run a high school.

If somebody says, "Go ask the principal," we will know that they are directing us to you. If somebody says, "The principal said it is okay," we will know that they are referring to you. If somebody says, "That is a matter for the principal," we will know that whatever that thing is, it requires your attention.

However, even though the *title*, high school principal, tells us a lot about you, and even though the *title*, high school principal, tells us what you do, High School Principal is not your name. It is your *title*.

Your *title* tells people what you do. Your *title* provides people with information about you. Your *title* tells people what they can expect from you.

Accordingly, Elohiym, being one of God's *titles*, reveals what God does. Elohiym, being one of God's *titles*, provides some information about God. Elohiym, being one of God's *titles*, lets people know what we can expect from God.

For example, from His title Elohiym, we know that He is the Creator.

From His title Elohiym, we know that He uses Words to create things. From His title Elohiym, we know that He uses Words to change things. His title, Elohiym, reveals to us *what God does*. He creates things with Words, and He changes things with Words.

Elohiym is God's *title*, but Elohiym is *not* God's Name.

What about El Shaddai? El Shaddai is another *title* for God, which reveals what God does. El Shaddai is another of God's *titles*, which provides some information about God. El Shaddai is another of God's *titles*, which lets people know what we can expect from God.

For example, from His title El Shaddai, we can know that God is Our Source. From His title El Shaddai, we can know that God is The All-Sufficient One. And from His title El Shaddai, we can know that God is "the God *Who is More Than Enough*." His title, El Shaddai, reveals to us *what* God *does*. He nourishes. He nurses. He supplies. He pours out in abundance.

El Shaddai is God's *title*, but El Shaddai is *not* God's Name.

Thus, while your *title* provides us with information about what you do, it is your *name* that discloses *who you are*. Your *name* is more *personal* than your *title*. Whereas your title is generic, your *name* is *personal*.

Why do I say your title is generic? Because it is not specific to you. You are not the *only* principal. That's not specific to you. You are not the *only* licensed cosmetologist. That's not specific to you. You are not the *only* real estate agent. That's not specific to you.

#AWhole'NotherLevel

Those titles are generic. But your name is specific to you. Your title, attorney at law, is not on your birth certificate, but your name, "Matilda Mistletoe," is. Your title, heart surgeon, is not on your driver's license, but your name, "Tommy Taylortine," is.

God is not the only *elohiym*. There are "little" gods. He says in psalm eighty-two, verse six, and John, chapter ten, verse thirty-four, "you are elohiym [gods]." God is not the only source. Your employer is a source. Those titles are generic. But He is the only YHWH. His Name, YHWH, is *personal*. That's taking it to "a whole 'nother level."

When you give someone your *name*, you are giving that person permission to know something personal about you. When you give someone your *name*, you are giving that person access to some things about you that the people who just have your *title* do not have. When you give someone your *name*, you are inviting that person to come in closer to you than those who just have your *title* are able to come. When you give someone your *name*, that's taking it to "a whole 'nother level."

The fact that God decided to disclose His *Name* to us is an indication that God wants us to know more about Him than just what a *title* tells us. The fact God decided to disclose His *Name* to us is an indication that God desires a personal relationship with us. The fact God decided to disclose His *Name* to us is an indication that God desires an intimate relationship with us. The fact God decided to disclose His *Name* to us is an indication that God wants us to take it to "a whole 'nother level."

God wants you to understand that even though He used Abraham to reconnect with mankind, He wants a closer connection to you. God wants you to understand that even though Isaac was the vehicle through whom the covenant would materialize, He wants a one-on-one relationship with you. God wants you to understand that even though Jacob was the channel through which the promises would manifest, God had intimacy with you in mind all the while. God desires an up-close, tight, intimate, personal relationship with you and with me.

And so when we get back over here into our text, God says to Moses, "Prior to this time, prior to now, any time I had appeared to Abraham or to Isaac or to Jacob, I had only let them know Me by My title. But I am about to take you to "a whole 'nother level." I am about to let you come up close to Me. I am YHWH."

Now let me provide a bit of context. This particular exchange occurred between YHWH and Moses around the time God had commissioned Moses to tell the pharaoh to let His people go. At least 400 years prior to that, Joseph had been appointed by the pharaoh of his day to rule over all of Egypt. Joseph subsequently moved Jacob and all of the children of Israel from Canaan to Egypt in order to provide for them because of a very severe famine that had swallowed up the land. The Bible says that at that time, when Jacob settled in Egypt, there was a total of seventy of them living in Egypt. But if we fast forward to Moses's time, some 430 years later, after Israel and Joseph and the pharaoh of Joseph's day had passed, the children of Israel had grown in number to about 600,000 men, not counting their children. And by this time, they had been made slaves in Egypt.

So, God chose Moses and raised him up to deliver a message to the contemporary pharaoh of Moses's day, which was "Let My people go." Moses was instructed to go to the pharaoh and tell him that he was sent by YHWH, the God of Abraham, Isaac, and Jacob, to bring the children of Israel out of Egypt, out of the house of bondage.

But Pharaoh's response was, "Who is YHWH that I should obey His voice to let Israel go? I do not know YHWH, nor will I let Israel go" (see Exodus 5:2). And after that, God determined, "When I finish with Pharaoh, he will know Who YHWH is, and when I finish with Pharaoh, he will let My people go."

And so, as I prepare to close out this chapter, I want to talk about Who YHWH is.

YHWH is the personal Name of God. YHWH is the Name that the Jews would not even utter because they interpreted Exodus, chapter twenty, verse seven, very narrowly. They interpreted, "You shall not take the Name of the Lord in vain" to mean you are not even supposed to speak His Name. Thus, in order to safeguard what they thought was this commandment, the Jews left out the vowels when they wrote the Name, and whenever they spoke the Name, instead of saying YHWH, they substituted in its place the title, *Adoni*, which is Hebrew for "Lord."

Nevertheless, YHWH is His personal Name. Yet, because there is no record of the vowels that they removed from the writings that depicted His Name, we cannot be 100 percent sure of the pronunciation. That's why some say *Yahweh*, and some say *Yehovah*, and some even say *Jehovah*.

But even though we cannot be 100 percent certain of the pronunciation of His Name, we are certain of what His Name means. In Exodus, chapter three, verses thirteen and fourteen, the Scripture says:

> Then Moses said to God, "Indeed, when I come to the children of Israel and say to them, 'The God of your fathers has sent me to you,' and they say to me, 'What is His [N]ame?' what shall I say to them?"

> And God said to Moses, "I AM WHO I
> AM." And He said, "Thus you shall say
> to the children of Israel, 'I AM has sent
> me to you.'"
>
> Exodus 3:13-14

YHWH means "I Am that I Am." *YHWH* means "I am too big to be compartmentalized." *YHWH* means "I am too vast to be articulated with words." *YHWH* means "I am too much to comprehend with your mind." Just tell them, "I Am that I Am." Just tell them "I Am" has sent you.

When I think of the Name YHWH, I think of its multifaceted nature, like a diamond. If you hold a diamond in the light and begin to adjust your vantage point, the diamond will show you different things. It will sparkle in different ways. It will glisten with different colors. As you turn it and move it about in the light, you will see different things come from it that you have never seen before. That's a good way to describe YHWH. YHWH is multi-faceted.

And although we occasionally refer to the titles of God and the facets and dimensions of YHWH all generically as the "Names of God," He has but one Name: His Name is YHWH. The titles are not His Name, they are titles that describe Him. And the facets and dimensions that we will explore in this book are not additional names. They are varying revelations of the single Name, YHWH.

So, Who is YHWH? YHWH is the Alpha and the Omega. YHWH is the Beginning and the End. YHWH is the First and the Last. YHWH is too much to describe.

YHWH is whoever you need Him to be. YHWH is bread when you are hungry. YHWH is water when you are thirsty. YHWH is a shelter in the time of storm.

#AWhole'NotherLevel

YHWH is more than we can fathom. YHWH is whatever you need at any given time. YHWH is the healer of the wounded, the restorer of the broken, peace for the worried, rest for the weary. YHWH is the Great "I AM."

YHWH is constantly revealing Himself, and YHWH always shows up to meet the need, just in the nick of time.

YHWH is the amazing God Who is more than wonderful.

YHWH is the lily of the valley and the bright morning star.

YHWH is the King of all kings and the Lord of all lords.

YHWH is the ever revealing, all-powerful, all-knowing God of Covenant.

Jesus said, "After this manner pray, say, 'Hallowed be Your Name.'" If we want the manifestation of what the Name entails, we've got to hallow the Name. If we want the manifestation of what the Name promises, then we have to hallow the Name. When we hallow the Name, we sow the Name. And the way we sow the Name is to speak the Name.

We thank You, oh God, that You are YHWH. We bless You that You are the ever-reveling God of Covenant. We honor You and exalt You, that You are the Most High God, Who desires an intimate relationship with Your people. You are YHWH. We hallow and reverence Your Name.

CHAPTER 10

YHWH-T'SIDKENU—THE LORD OUR RIGHTEOUSNESS

#TradingPlaces

Exodus, chapter twenty, verse seven, states:

> "You shall not take the Name of the LORD your God in vain, for the LORD will not hold him guiltless who takes His Name in vain" (Exodus 20:7).

I think it is important for us to note that this is not a casual recommendation. God is not leaving us with a choice or an option. This is not "if you want to…" This is not a suggestion that you can follow "if it suits your fancy."

Here, God is speaking to His people, and He is talking to us about how we carry or transport His Name. God is commanding us not to waste His Name but to carry His Name purposefully. We are being challenged to use the Name of the Lord as a tool like a carpenter uses his hammer and nails to build a set of kitchen cabinets. We are being challenged to use

God's Name like a seed, recognizing the kingdom principle that God put the power in the seed to make itself come to pass.

This kingdom principle relates to the other passage of Scripture that we have been using as a foundation for this teaching, which comes from the Gospel of St. Luke, chapter eleven, verse two:

He said to them, "When you pray, say: Our Father in heaven, Hallowed be Your Name" (Luke 11:2).

In the last few chapters, as we have chiseled away at what it means to "hallow" the Name, we noted that to hallow the Name is to sow the Name and to sow the Name is to hallow the Name. We have further concluded that the way to sow the Name is to speak the Name.

And because God put the power in the Word to make itself come to pass, when you talk to Him about Who He says He is, you are sowing the seed to make that very thing come to pass in your life.

In the last chapter, we took a look at *YHWH*, the personal Name of God. When God talked to Moses, He told him, "I am drawing you in, closer to Me than even Abraham, Isaac, and Jacob ever were. I never told them My Name. But I don't just want religion from you, I want a relationship with you, so I am telling you My Name."

Nevertheless, even though God disclosed His Name to demonstrate His desire for intimacy with His people, *YHWH* is the Name that the Jews would not even utter because they interpreted Exodus, chapter twenty, verse seven, very narrowly. They interpreted, "You shall not take the Name of the Lord in vain…" to mean you are not even supposed to speak His Name.

But why would God give them His Name if He did not want them to speak it? And why would Jesus tell us to "hallow" His Name if He did not want us to know it? That defies logic. Nevertheless, that's how the Jews interpreted that commandment. So, in order to avoid violating what they thought was this commandment, the Jews left out the vowels when they wrote the Name; and whenever they spoke the Name, instead of saying YHWH, they substituted in its place the title, *Adoni*, which is Hebrew for "Lord."

Nevertheless, YHWH is His personal Name.

And *YHWH* means "You cannot define Me. I Am that I Am." *YHWH* means "I am too big to fit in your box." *YHWH* means "I am too comprehensive for you to figure out." *YHWH* means "I am too powerful for you to withstand." *YHWH* means, "Whatever you need Me to be, that's Who I Am. I Am that I Am. I Am YHWH."

In the last chapter, I addressed the multi-faceted nature of YHWH. When I think of all the angles of YHWH, I liken His nature to a diamond. If you hold a diamond in the light and begin to adjust your vantage point, the diamond will show you different things. It will sparkle in different ways. It will glisten with different colors. As you turn it and move it about in the light, you will see different things come from it that you have never seen before. Like a diamond, YHWH is multi-faceted.

Here in this chapter, I want to look at one of those facets or one of those angles of YHWH. For that purpose, let's go first, to 2 Corinthians, chapter five, and second, to Jeremiah, chapter twenty-three.

> "For He made Him [W]ho knew no sin to be sin for us, that we might become the righteousness of God in Him" (2 Corinthians 5:21).

#TradingPlaces

"In His days Judah will be saved, And Israel will dwell safely; Now this is His Name by which He will be called: THE LORD OUR RIGHTEOUSNESS [*YHWH-Tsidkenu*]" (Jeremiah 23:6).

In this chapter, we are going to look at what God revealed as one of those facets of our multi-faceted YHWH. We want to talk about *YHWH-T'Sidkenu*, the Lord our *Righteousness*. He traded places with us.

Trading Places is a 1983 comedy that stars Dan Aykroyd as an upper-class commodities broker and Eddie Murphy as a poor street hustler, whose lives cross when they are made the subjects of an elaborate bet to test how each man would perform when their life circumstances are swapped. Thus, Murphy's character becomes the commodities broker, and Akroyd's character is forced to take on the lifestyle of an impoverished societal outcast. In this movie, Eddie Murphy's character gets to rise to the top of the economic echelon, but this happens at the expense of Dan Akroyd's character.

In the twenty-first verse of 2 Corinthians, chapter five, which is one of the reference scriptures that we just read, the Bible says, "For He made Him [W]ho knew no sin to be sin for us, that we might become the righteousness of God in Him."

That's trading places. He took on our sin and gave us His righteousness.

We are talking about one of YHWH's many facets that He has decided to reveal to us: that is, YHWH-T'Sidkenu, the Lord our Righteousness.

It is important to note from the outset that righteousness is a *big deal* with God. The cornerstone of our relationship with God is righteousness. Righteousness is necessary in order to access God. Righteousness is necessary in order to engage the presence of God in our midst. Righteousness is required in order to get God involved in our circumstances. Righteousness is the gateway to the blessings of God. Again, righteousness a *big deal* with God.

Well, what is *righteousness*? How are we defining this "righteousness" that is such a big deal to God? Righteousness bespeaks the conduct of mankind that is acceptable to God, such as integrity, virtue, purity of life, rightness, and correctness of thinking, feeling, and acting.

In other words, righteousness is about how we act, and righteousness is about how we think, and righteousness is about the condition of our hearts. These things matter to God. Because we were created in His image and after His likeness, we are supposed to reflect God. Because we were created in His image and after His likeness, we are supposed to act like God.

But the problem we have is that because sin entered the world, we do not reflect God as we should, and because sin contaminated the world, we do not act like God though we should.

This is one of those "straits betwixt two" that we see in the Bible. Paul at one time spoke of being in a "strait betwixt two." In other words, that is talking about a dilemma. These issues regarding how the contamination of sin undermines God's demands for His people to reflect Him and act like Him happens to be one of those "straits betwixt two."

Now let me just make a few observations here.

1. It is undisputed that God wants a relationship with His people. In 2 Corinthians, chapter six, verse sixteen, the Bible says, "For you are the temple of the living God. As God has said: 'I will dwell in them and walk among

#TradingPlaces

them. I will be their God, and they shall be My people'"
(2 Corinthians 6:16).

Thus, from the creation of time, God has wanted a
relationship with His people.

2. A relationship with God, however, requires righteousness. Having grown up in church, I have heard many a
sermon stating that, "None but the righteous shall see
God." Well, remember, Adam was ejected out of Eden
and out of the presence of God because of sin. And
remember what God said to Moses when He spoke to
him from that burning bush? "Take your shoes off your
feet, for the ground on which you stand is Holy!" (see
Exodus 3:4-6).

The fact that God requires righteousness from a
people who have been contaminated with sin presents
a paradox.

3. Now, let me talk about the fact that there exists a "Paradox
of Righteousness." A paradox is a statement that, despite
apparently sound reasoning from true premises, leads to
a self-contradictory or a logically unacceptable conclusion. Something, such as a situation, that is made up of
two opposite things and seems impossible but is actually
true or possible is a paradox. Some illustrations are:

- Your enemy's friend is your enemy.
- I am nobody.
- "What a pity that youth must be wasted on
  the young."
- Wise fool.

With respect to the issue of righteousness, the paradox is this: on the one hand, God requires righteousness as noted in Matthew, chapter five:

> Whoever therefore breaks one of the least of these commandments, and teaches men so, shall be called least in the kingdom of heaven; but whoever does and teaches them, he shall be called great in the kingdom of heaven. For I say to you, that unless your righteousness exceeds the righteousness of the scribes and Pharisees, you will by no means enter the kingdom of heaven.
>
> Matthew 5:19-20

But on the other hand, in our best efforts, we fall short of that righteousness.

"There is none righteous, no, not one..." (Romans 3:10).

Moreover, righteousness is not something we can obtain of our own volition, or by our own power, or in the flesh. Why? Because the best we can offer falls short of God's standards for righteousness.

Isaiah, chapter sixty-four, says, "But we are all like an unclean thing, And all our righteousnesses are like filthy rags" (Isaiah 64:6).

Thus, the paradox is this: even though we fall short in our attempts to *do* righteousness, we have been *made* righteous. Even though we cannot do righteousness, we

#TradingPlaces

are the righteousness of God in Christ Jesus. The next question we need to address is, how do we get there?

4. Because of this paradox, the way we get there is through *reckoning* or *imputation*.

Way back in the day, in my accounting class, I was taught that when the books don't balance, you need a "plug," a reconciliation, a reckoning, an imputation. The purpose of the plug is to fill in the gap and bring books into balance that otherwise would not balance. Likewise, in order for us to meet God's standards for righteousness, there must be a "plug," a reconciliation, a reckoning, an act of imputation. And the Bible lets us know that this comes by faith.

Speaking of Abraham, the Scripture says, "And he believed in the Lord, and He accounted ["counted," KJV; "credited," NASB] it to him for righteousness" (Genesis 15:6).

In other words, God has to do it.

Regarding what happened to Abraham, as described in Genesis, chapter fifteen, verse six, the translation varies across a few different versions of the Bible. One translation says, "God accounted it." One translation says, "God counted it." Another translation says, "God credited it." A cross-reference from the twenty-second verse of Romans, chapter four, says, "It was imputed to him." The bottom line is that God has to do it.

In 2 Corinthians, chapter five, verse twenty-one, the Bible says, "For He made Him [W]ho knew no sin to be sin for us, that we might become the righteousness of God in Him" (2 Corinthians 5:21).

In other words, He traded places with us. He took on our sin. And God gave us His righteousness. He is YHWH-T'Sidkenu, He is the Lord our Righteousness.

Christ became our reckoning agent. Christ became our plug. He is the agent of our imputation. And how did He do this? By trading places with us.

The Bible says in Romans, chapter eight, "There is therefore now no condemnation to those who are in Christ Jesus [...because] the law of the Spirit of life in Christ Jesus has made [us] free from the law of sin and death" (Romans 8:1-2).

On account of this righteousness, we have been reconnected to God. And on account of this righteousness, we have access to God. And on account of this righteousness, we have been restored to our place at the table of God. And on account of that righteousness, we can receive from God.

Thus, Who is YHWH? YHWH is too much to describe. Who is YHWH? YHWH is whoever you need Him to be. He is YHWH-T'Sidkenu, the Lord our Righteousness.

So, when the devil tries to tell you that you are not worthy, you can say, "Get behind me, Satan, because He traded places with me, and He is YHWH-T'Sidkenu, the Lord my Righteousness."

And when the devil tries to bring up your past, you can say, "I rebuke you, Satan; God is not mad at me. He traded places with me, and He is YHWH-T'Sidkenu, the Lord my Righteousness."

And when the devil tries to arrest you in guilt and condemnation and make you think you don't deserve what God promised you in His Word, you can say, "I resist you, Satan. God Himself traded places with me, and He is YHWH-T'Sidkenu, the Lord my Righteousness."

#TradingPlaces

He is YHWH-T'Sidkenu. He traded places with you. And He is the Lord your Righteousness, and you are the righteousness of God in Christ Jesus.

And because He is your YHWH-T'Sidkenu, when God looks at you, He doesn't see you. When God looks at you, He sees Christ in you, the hope of glory.

Jesus said, "After this manner pray, say, 'Hallowed be Your Name.'" If we want the manifestation of what the Name entails, we've got to hallow the Name. If we want the manifestation of what the Name promises, we have to hallow the Name. When we hallow the Name, we sow the Name. And the way we sow the Name is to speak the Name.

I thank You, oh God, that You are YHWH-T'Sidkenu. Thank You that You are the Lord my Righteousness. Thank You that You cleansed me in spite of myself. Thank You that You washed me in spite of myself. Thank You that You restored me in spite of myself. And You told me that if I seek first the kingdom of God and Your righteousness, everything that I need and everything that I want will always automatically be added to me.

You are YHWH-T'Sidkenu, and I am righteous in Your sight. Therefore, I have access to You. Therefore, I can come boldly before the throne of grace to obtain mercy and find grace to help in time of need. Thank You that I don't have to come cowering like a little dog with his tail tucked between his legs. But I have been restored in You, and everything that you promised me in Your Word is mine. Thank You that I can claim it. Thank You that I can expect it. Thank You that I can walk with my head held high. And thank You that I can even demand it, in Jesus's Name.

You traded places with me. You have made me worthy. You are YHWH-T'Sidkenu, the Lord my Righteousness.

DR. MELVIN G. BARNEY, ESQ.

CHAPTER 11

YHWH-M'KADDESH—THE LORD OUR SANCTIFIER

#God'sProperty

You know the routine now. We have two foundation scriptures for this teaching. The first comes from Exodus, chapter twenty, verse seven, which reads: "You shall not take the Name of the LORD your God in vain, for the LORD will not hold him guiltless who takes His Name in vain" (Exodus 20:7).

We have learned that we should use the Name of the Lord as a tool like a mechanic uses his wrench to tighten the nuts and bolts on the vehicle on which he is working. And we are learning to recognize that God's Name is like a seed, which, when sown and watered and tended, reproduces after its kind, because God put the power in the Name to make itself come to pass.

For several chapters, we have reiterated what it means to "hallow the Name." When we hallow the Name, we are sowing the Name. And to sow the Name is to hallow the Name. The way we sow the Name is by speaking the Name.

It is by speaking the Name that we usher in the power of God to manifest the promise, because God put the power in the Name to make itself come to pass. This is a kingdom principle. Jesus Christ said, "The kingdom of God is as if a man should scatter seed on the ground."

This is a kingdom principle, and it tells us how the kingdom of God operates. Now let's review our second foundation scripture, which is St. Luke, chapter eleven, verse two, where Jesus provides a model for putting this Kingdom Principle into practice: "He said to them, 'When you pray, say: Our Father in heaven, Hallowed be Your Name'" (Luke 11:2).

In Chapters 7 and 8, we were introduced, respectively, to Elohiym, God the Creator, and El Shaddai, the Almighty God Who Is More Than Enough, both of which are titles for God, but neither is His Name. It is good to know these titles because they tell us what God does. However, because God wanted more for us and desires an intimate relationship with us, He went further and gave us His Name.

It was in Chapter 9 that we got a revelation that YHWH is the personal Name of God. And if you want to know what YHWH means, think, "I Am that I Am," because YHWH is multi-faceted. There are multiple dimensions to YHWH. He has many facets and many angles. Every time you think you know how He's going to move, He shows you something else. You expect Him to lay hands on you, but He speaks the Word over you instead. You expect Him to speak the Word over you, but He touches you instead. You expect Him to touch you, but He spits in your eyes instead. He is YHWH. Don't try to box Him. Don't try to explain Him. Don't try to instruct Him. Just let Him be God. He is YHWH.

And like a diamond that exposes many things about itself as you move it about in the light, YHWH is multi-faceted. So at this time, I want to look at another of the facets or of the angles of YHWH, which we can explore by going over to Leviticus, chapter twenty, and examining verses seven and eight.

> Consecrate yourselves therefore, and be holy, for I am the Lord your God. And you shall keep My statutes, and perform them: I am the Lord [W]ho sanctifies you. [*YHWH-M'Kaddeshkem*].
> Leviticus 20:7-8

Sanctification is one of many "churchy" words and "churchy" concepts that we don't often hear outside of "churchy" contexts. Why is that? Well, the reason is that the concept of sanctification relates exclusively to God, to God's ways, and to God's stuff. Sanctification is a God's thing, so it would only come up in areas that involve God, God's stuff, God's property.

And depending on what side of the "church railroad tracks" you grew up on, the very mention of this word can leave a good taste in your mouth, or it can leave a very bitter taste in your mouth.

For those who grew up on one side of the "church railroad tracks," the concept of sanctification and the notion of being sanctified is a source of great celebration and vigor and spiritual pride and esteem: to understand that we are God's chosen; to understand that we are God's favorite; to understand that we are the apple of God's eyes; to understand that God looks out for us; to understand that God lays out the land for us; to understand that God will move mountains for us. This is the source of great celebration. Much rejoicing. Spiritual pride. Bounties of esteem.

#God'sProperty

But if you grew up on the other side of the "church railroad tracks," just hearing the words "sanctification" or "sanctified" is a turn-off. When those people hear the word "sanctification," they shut down. When they hear the word "sanctified," they get images of long dresses that go down to the ankles and blouses that cover the neck. They get the image of a wardrobe that consists only of black and white. They get the image of men going to the beach, not in beach attire but fully dressed in their black suits—at the beach.

When those people hear the word "sanctified," all that comes to their mind is a list of "don'ts" and "can'ts." Don't go to the movies. Can't wear certain colors, like red. Don't play sports or participate in gym. Can't wear make-up or lipstick.

A lot of people who grew up on that side of the "church railroad tracks" actually developed a hostility toward the church, many developed a distaste for the church, and many want nothing to do with the church because to them, "sanctification" amounted exclusively to a bunch of "don'ts" and "can'ts."

In this chapter, I want to clear up some of the confusion and talk about what our sanctification is really about.

For that purpose, I want to go to 1 Peter, chapter two, verse nine, which reads as follows:

> But you are a chosen generation, a royal priesthood, a holy nation, His own special people [a peculiar people, KJV], that you may proclaim the praises of Him [W]ho called you out of darkness into His marvelous light.
>
> 1 Peter 2:9

Speaking to God's people, those who God has sanctified, the Scripture says that you are a *chosen* generation. That means you are hand-picked. That means you are significant. That means you are important. That means you are special. You are chosen by God. God has made you distinct. God has made you distinguished. God has made you different. God has made you stand out from all the rest. That verse in the KJV says you are "peculiar," and that is meant in a good way. We are "peculiar" in that we are God's property. We are God's purchased possession. We belong to Him. We are God's property.

This speaks of *YHWH-M'Kaddesh*, the Lord our *Sanctifier*. But before I get too far into this, I want to circle back to look at this in Hebrew: *YHWH-M'Kaddesh*. It is the *M'Kaddesh* part that addresses the business about being "sanctified" and what that "churchy" word really means.

Now let me point out that some of you may have come across different tenses or conjugations of the word. You may have seen it written *M'Kaddeshcum* or *M'Koddishkem* or something like that. There are a few reasons for this. Remember, we are translating from Hebrew, and the Hebrew alphabet is comprised of letters and vowels that are different from English.

Thus, one explanation for spelling differences is because we sound the Hebrew word out, trying to match the sound and assigning English letters to the sound. Another reason you will find differences is because of conjugation or tense or mood or something like that, so that has to do with how the word is used. We know in English that sometimes the tense changes the structure of words. Depending on the person, conjugation, and tense, *to look* becomes "look," "look(s)," "looked," "looking," "will look," etc. Another example is the verb *to be*. Depending on the tense, *to be* becomes "am/are,"

#God'sProperty

"are," "is/are," "was/were," "were," "am being/are being/is being," "will be," etc. Lots of rules. Well, Hebrew has its rules as well.

And under the Hebrew rules, *M'Kaddeshcum* or *M'Koddishkem* translates as "the Lord Who sanctifies you." But I don't want to get hung up on the spelling differences or the tense, or the way it may have been conjugated or the context. I want to focus on what it means.

The Hebrew root word is *kodesh*, which, depending on the context, is translated as "holy," or "consecrated," or "dedicated," or "sanctified," and that means "apartness," "set-apartness," "separateness." It speaks to a distinction or a difference, where the thing described is different or distinguishable from the rest. This word, *kodesh*, describes God.

So let me ask the question: who is like the Lord? Nobody. Nothing. Not one. There is none like Him. He is different. He is distinct. He is apart from the norm. He is separate from the crowd. He is different from the rest. He is *holy*. And that's what *kodesh* means. When you think about it, the state of being *holy* is an attribute that can be assigned only to God.

Yet, even though only God is *kodesh*, He tells us to be *kodesh*. (I feel a *deja vu* moment coming on. I feel a Groundhog Day moment coming on here. This is another one of those "straits betwixt two" moments like we talked about in Chapter 10. This is another one of those paradoxes, like we talked about in the previous chapter.)

In the scripture we read, over in Leviticus, chapter twenty, the Bible says, "Consecrate yourselves therefore, and be holy." The KJV says, "Sanctify yourselves therefore, and be ye holy." Remember, the same word *kodesh* that is translated as "consecrate" in the NKJV is translated as "sanctify" in the KJV. Thus, in this context, "consecrate" equals "sanctify."

DR. MELVIN G. BARNEY, ESQ.

The paradox is that He is telling us to be *holy* (*kodesh*) even though only God is *holy* (*kodesh*).

> Consecrate yourselves therefore, and be holy, for I am the Lord your God. And you shall keep My statutes, and perform them: I am the Lord [W]ho sanctifies you. [YHWH-M'Kaddeshkem].
>
> Leviticus 20:7-8

The natural question that follows is this: how can we be holy if God alone is holy? The way we have been made holy is the same way we became righteous. God did it. Look at what it says in Leviticus, chapter twenty, and how that seventh verse ends: He says, "I am the Lord Who sanctifies you" (that's *YHWH-M'Kaddeshkem*). "*I* am the One Who does it. You didn't do it, *I* did."

When God saved us and cleansed us and washed us, He hand-picked us and chose us; He separated us and made us distinct; He distinguished us from everybody else and made us different from all the rest. *Kodesh* describes Him and Him alone, so by sanctifying us, God made us like Him. He is YHWH-M'Kaddesh, He is the Lord Who made us holy. He is YHWH-M'Kaddesh, the Lord our Sanctifier.

And because God did it, it is done. Because He chose me, I am chosen. Because He separated me, I am separate. Because He set me apart, I am set apart. Because He distinguished me, I am distinct. He is YHWH-M'Kaddeshkem. He is the Lord Who *sanctifies us.*

The image that I get when I think about this concept of sanctification is like what you do with a possession that is important to you, significant to you, meaningful to you, and precious to you. What do you do? You sanctify it. You

#God'sProperty

administer special attention to it that you don't administer to the rest. You give it special care that you don't give to the rest. You pay special attention to it that you do not pay to the rest. Why? Because you have sanctified it.

Some of you, women, for example, have your everyday jewelry, the items you bought from Kmart, or that you got from Walmart. It may have come from the endcaps at Target while you were waiting in the checkout line. I'm talking about your costume jewelry, your everyday jewelry. By the way, isn't it something how, when you saw it in the store, it looked so good, but when you got it home…

Anyway, that's the everyday costume jewelry that you don't really care about. That's what you take off at the end of the day and toss it on the dresser. That's the stuff that, if it gets tangled, you don't really trip. That's what that may end up on the floor or get lost, but you don't really care. Why? Because it is not that important to you. It is not that valuable to you. You know you can just run to Walmart and get another if you want another. It does not really matter to you.

But you also have some jewelry that matters very much to you. It may be a family heirloom that was passed down for several generations. It may be a gift that you received from a special somebody. It may be a costly, expensive, or priceless piece of jewelry that is very important to you.

Now you don't treat this heirloom the same as the costume jewelry. You don't break out the pearls every day like you do the pieces you got from Walmart. You don't even store your precious jewels in the same place as the rest of the items that you just toss on the dresser. You have a special place that you keep the precious jewels. You take special care of the heirlooms. You sanctify the expensive gems and make a difference because they are important to you.

Some of you, brethren, have more than one car. One might be your everyday run-around car that you don't keep very clean; you don't do a lot to it. You leave it parked outside because it is not that valuable to you. You don't take it to the car wash very often, because it is not a big deal to you. But that Lamborghini, that one is rare, that one is expensive, that one cost you a lot. Everybody knows not to bring any food into that car. You'd better not catch a bird...

That car gets washed every week. You would not think about leaving that car outside or parking it on the street like the other. That car is garage kept. You have set that car apart. That car is sanctified.

And this is what God has done for you. You are sanctified. You are set apart. You are God's precious heirloom. You are valuable to Him. God looks out for you. God sees you differently from the rest. God has set you apart from the others. He is YHWH-M'Kaddesh. He is the Lord our Sanctifier.

And because God has sanctified you, God takes care of you. Because God has sanctified you, God looks out for you. Because God has sanctified you, God protects you. Because God has sanctified you, God preserves you. He is YHWH-M'Kaddesh. He is the Lord our Sanctifier.

That's why you can have peace in the midst of a pandemic because you know Him as YHWH-M'Kaddesh, the Lord our Sanctifier. That's why you can have peace in the midst of a raging inferno because you know Him as YHWH-M'Kaddesh, the Lord our Sanctifier. That's why you can be calm, cool, and collected when everybody around you is pulling out their hair because you know Him as YHWH-M'Kaddesh, the Lord our Sanctifier. You don't have to worry about anything, and you can be careful about nothing because you know Him as YHWH-M'Kaddesh, the Lord our Sanctifier. You do not have to fear anything but

#God'sProperty

walk in authority over the enemy because you know Him as YHWH-M'Kaddesh, the Lord our Sanctifier. You are in this world but not of this world. You are sanctified. You are the light of the world. This world would be a dark, grim place but for you. But it's not, not while you are here because God has sanctified you.

Remember the days of Noah? Like Noah, who was preserved in that ark from the flood that would destroy the earth, you have been sanctified and, therefore, are protected and preserved from the things that are going on in the world. As a matter of fact, you are the salt of the earth. This world would rot and decay but for you. But it can't. Not while you are here because God has sanctified you. Remember Sodom and Gomorrah? God said, "If I find ten righteous folks in the land, I will not destroy it for the sake of the ten." He is YHWH-M'Kaddesh, the Lord our Sanctifier.

If you have been saved, God has sanctified you. And since He has sanctified you, He expects you to act like it.

You are a chosen generation, a royal priesthood, a holy nation, God's special people, who have a responsibility to demonstrate His praises, who have a responsibility to demonstrate His power.

You have been sanctified, and you need to act like it. He said you are a royal priesthood. You cannot act like a commoner. Royalty needs to act like royalty. And you need to act like you are sanctified.

I don't care how hard you try, there is no way you are going to get a five-carat diamond to act like cubic zirconium. You can set that five-carat in a pile of cubic zirconia, and it will stick out like a sore thumb. Why? Because it is different. There is no way you can get it to tone down its sparkle like cubic zirconium. When the light hits it, it will stick out. It is different. It is sanctified.

I don't care how hard you try, there is no way you are going to get a Rolls Royce to act like a Ford Pinto. You can surround that Rolls Royce with Fords, but it is always going to stick out because it is different. There is no way you can make it sound like a Ford Pinto; when you start that engine, it will stick out. It is different. It is sanctified.

And God says, "Since I have sanctified you, you need to act like it. Since I have brought you out of darkness, you need to act like it. Since I have redeemed you, you ought to act like it. Since I have set you on high, you ought to act like it."

> But you are a chosen generation, a royal priesthood, a holy nation, His own special people, that you may proclaim the praises of Him [W]ho called you out of darkness into His marvelous light.
>
> 1 Peter 2:9

So Who is YHWH? YHWH is too much to describe. Who is YHWH? YHWH is whoever you need Him to be.

He is YHWH-M'Kaddesh, He is the Lord our Sanctifier.

So when the devil tries to tell you that you are going under, you know that's a lie because He is YHWH-M'Kaddesh. He is the Lord Who Sanctifies you.

And when the devil tries to tell you that God does not care about you, you know that's a lie because He is YHWH-M'Kaddesh. He is the Lord Who Sanctifies you.

And when the devil tries to make you feel like God has left you, you know that's a lie because He is YHWH-M'Kaddesh. He is the Lord Who Sanctifies you.

Jesus said, "After this manner pray, say 'Hallowed be Your Name.'" If we want the manifestation of what the Name entails, we've got to hallow the Name. If we want the

#God'sProperty

manifestation of what the Name promises, we have to hallow the Name. When we hallow the Name, we sow the Name. And the way we sow the Name is to speak the Name.

We thank You, oh God, that You are YHWH-M'Kaddesh. You are the Lord our Sanctifier.

Thank You that I get to be a chosen generation. Thank You for setting me apart. Thank You, YHWH-M'Kaddesh, that You don't see me as common, but You have made me distinctive. Thank You, YHWH-M'Kaddesh, that You have made me a royal priesthood. I am royalty. I am a child of the Most High God. Thank You, YHWH-M'Kaddesh, for making me the light of the world. Thank You for making me the salt of the earth. Thank You, YHWH-M'Kaddesh, for making me a part of a distinct race of people who get to demonstrate Your glory. Thank You for making me a peculiar people. I am distinguished. I am different. I am set apart. I am special to You. And You are YHWH-M'Kaddesh, You are the Lord Who sanctifies me.

CHAPTER 12

YHWH-SHALOM—THE LORD OUR PEACE

#HeCompletesYou

Exodus, chapter twenty, states: "You shall not take the Name of the LORD your God in vain, for the LORD will not hold him guiltless who takes His Name in vain" (Exodus 20:7).

In Luke, chapter eleven, verse two, Jesus is speaking: "He said to them, 'When you pray, say: Our Father in heaven, Hallowed be Your Name'" (Luke 11:2).

While "hallowing" is not a part of our everyday speech, we have come to understand what it means to "hallow the Name." Moreover, we have learned that when we "hallow" or "sanctify" the Name, we are sowing the Name, that to sow the Name is to "hallow" or "sanctify" the Name, and the way we sow the Name is by speaking the Name. It is by speaking the Name that we usher in the power of God to manifest the promise because God put the power in the Name to make itself come to pass. This is a kingdom principle. Jesus Christ said, "The kingdom of God is as if a man should scatter seed on the ground."

It goes without saying that there is a lot of confusion that surrounds what God expects His people to do with His Name. God wants us to understand that His Name is not some cute pendant that we wear around our neck or a pretty little charm that we dangle from our wrist. The Name of the Lord is a powerful resource that we have at our disposal to usher the power of God into our lives.

We should not for a minute take lightly the fact that God has given us access to His personal Name, nor for the fact that He is constantly revealing Himself to us by means of His Name. YHWH means I Am that I Am, and like a diamond, He is constantly revealing and displaying different dimensions and facets and angles of His multi-faceted nature.

He said, "I Am That I Am." You are looking for Him to move one way, and He does something different. He can feed your household for years with a cup of oil and a handful of cornmeal. He can pay off all of your debt and set you up in a business with some pots & pans that you borrow from your neighbors. He can take a little boy's filet-o-fish sandwich and feed five thousand men plus their wives plus their children. He is YHWH. Don't try to box Him. Don't try to confine Him. Don't try to instruct Him. Just let Him be God. He is YHWH.

In this chapter, we are going to explore yet another facet of YHWH, introduced in Judges, chapter six: "Then the Lord said to him, 'Peace be with you; do not fear, you shall not die.' So Gideon built an altar there to the Lord, and called it the-Lord-Is-Peace [*YHWH-Shalom*]" (Judges 6:23-24).

In 1996, Gracie Films produced, and TriStar Pictures distributed *Jerry Maguire*, which starred Tom Cruise, Renée Zellweger, and Cuba Gooding Jr., and which was one of those movies that was riddled with famous lines that have stood the test of time. Cuba Gooding Jr. won an Oscar for his role as a professional football player on the last leg of his career, who made famous the line, "Show me the money." Renée Zellweger, who portrayed the love-starved wife of Jerry Maguire, made the line, "You had me at hello" famous. But hers was in response to the line made famous by Tom Cruise, who starred as Jerry Maguire, and who, after having his biggest day ever as a sports agent, came to the realization that though she had always been there for him, she was not present to enjoy the celebration, and he was left alone. So he crashed his wife's male-bashing party to toss out the famous line, "You complete me."

And that's what I want to draw from in order to talk about Who *YHWH-Shalom*, the Lord our *Peace*, is to us. He completes us.

If we were able to take a tram ride back into time and find ourselves in the Garden of Eden, back when God created Adam and set him in the midst of the garden, not only would we find ourselves in a place that is more beautiful than anything we can imagine, but we would find ourselves in another very unfamiliar environment: where there is a perfect state of peace. We do not know what it is like to be free of anxiety or worry or fear because, for us, those have become our norm. We do not have a clue of what it is like to be free of migraines, pressure, and stress because where we live, these are a part of life. We would feel like a fish out of water where there are no disturbances, or where there are no agitants, or where there is nobody getting on our nerves, because our days are full of disturbances, our lives are filled with agitants, and it seems like people are standing in line just to wear out our nerves.

But as outlandish and farfetched and foreign as it sounds, that was the environment in which God placed Adam and Eve at the start, and this was the will of God for them from the start, and the lifestyle of perfect peace was the

#HeCompletesYou

127

way of life for them from the start... Until they sinned; until they fell.

And once they sinned, once they fell, all of a sudden, it was as if they woke up in a nightmare. Now all of a sudden, they know fear and worry. Now all of a sudden, they are aware of themselves and able to be intimidated. Now all of a sudden, Adam and Eve feel stressed and need to hide from the One Whom, up to that point, they had only known as their life and their source, and the One Who took care of them, looked after them, had fun with them, and loved them. Now all of a sudden, they feel alienated from the God Who, just yesterday, was their best friend.

But the will of God for His people then is the same as the will of God for His people now: and that is to live in a perfect state of peace.

The very popular and widely known, if not universally known, Hebrew word is *shalom*. And everybody knows that *shalom* means "peace." But what people may not know is that *shalom* also means "wholeness" and "completeness." *Shalom* speaks to your soundness. It speaks to your well-being.

When we think about God's will for His people, it is important for you to understand that your well-being is God's will for you. God's will for you is peace. And whatever it takes to bring you into a state of peace, that's what God wants for you. God's will for you is wholeness and completeness—God does not want you broken or jacked up. Whatever is needful to make you whole, that's the will of God for you. God wants to complete you. He is YHWH-Shalom, He is the Lord our Peace. He completes you.

And the Word of God is full of indicators that God's will for His people is peace. The Bible is filled with encounters where the Lord encourages His people to not be in fear and to not worry and to not fret. God wants you in peace.

DR. MELVIN G. BARNEY, ESQ.

I touched on this a little earlier, but let me just double back and revisit how we got here. We have made the case that God's will for us is perfect peace, and that God wants us in peace, and that it is not God's will for us to be in fear, or to be anxiety-ridden, or to be worrying, or to be stressing out, or to be up all night scratching and itching, or to be breaking out in hives or welts about anything. Since these are not God's will for us, how did we get here? The answer is sin.

Let me just tarry here for a moment and point out some observations about the effects of Adam's sin on our *shalom* and what sin brought our way.

Observation 1: Sin brought alienation from God. Because of sin, Adam was kicked out of the presence of God.

In the only recorded admonition from God to Adam, God said, "Of the tree of the knowledge of good and evil you shall not eat, for in the day that you eat of it you shall surely die" (Genesis 2:17).

Observation 2: Sin brought destruction by God. Because of sin, God regretted having created man and sent a great flood to destroy the entire earth.

> Then the Lord saw that the wickedness of man was great in the earth, and that every intent of the thoughts of his heart was only evil continually. And the Lord was sorry that He had made man on the earth, and He was grieved in His heart. So the Lord said, "I will destroy man whom I have created from the face of the earth, both man and beast, creeping thing and birds of the air, for I am sorry that I have made them."
>
> Genesis 6:5-7

#HeCompletesYou

Observation 3: Sin brought the curses from God. Because of sin, God pronounced empowerment to fail and itemized a number of penalties for disobedience over those who sinned against Him.

> But it shall come to pass, if you do not obey the voice of the Lord your God, to observe carefully all His commandments and His statutes which I command you today, that all these curses will come upon you and overtake you [...] And your heavens which are over your head shall be bronze, and the earth which is under you shall be iron [...] So you shall be driven mad because of the sight which your eyes see [...] And among those nations you shall find no rest, nor shall the sole of your foot have a resting place; but there the Lord will give you a trembling heart, failing eyes, and anguish of soul. Your life shall hang in doubt before you; you shall fear day and night, and have no assurance of life. In the morning you shall say, "Oh, that it were evening!" And at evening you shall say, "Oh, that it were morning!" because of the fear which terrifies your heart, and because of the sight which your eyes see.
>
> Deuteronomy 28:15, 23, 34, 65-67

But the good news is that it did not stop there! The good news is that's not how the story ends. The good news is that God is sovereign and takes even the bad things in life and turns them for good to those who love Him...

What did God do? He wrapped Himself up in flesh and said, "Let Me go down there and fix this thing." Christ Himself became our bridge back to God.

> Christ has redeemed us from the curse of the law, having become a curse for us (for it is written, "Cursed is everyone who hangs on a tree"), that the blessing of Abraham might come upon the Gentiles in Christ Jesus, that we might receive the promise of the Spirit through faith.
>
> Galatians 3:13-14

And as a result, we now have...
peace with God,
peace of or from God,
peace like God.

Peace with God

First, we have "peace with God." What do I mean by peace with God? The Bible says in chapter five of the Epistle to the Romans, "Therefore, having been justified by faith, we have peace with God through our Lord Jesus Christ" (Romans 5:1).

Even though sin brought alienation, Christ brought reconciliation. Thus, there is no more alienation.

And even though sin brought destruction, Christ brought reconnection. Thus, there is no more destruction.

#HeCompletesYou

And even though sin brought the curses, Christ has redeemed us from those curses. Thus, there are no more curses.

Peace with God is by faith.

Peace of or from God

Second, as a result of what Christ did, we now have the "peace of or from God." What do I mean by the peace of or from God? The Bible says in Philippians, chapter four:

> Be anxious for nothing, but in everything by prayer and supplication, with thanks-giving, let your requests be made known to God; and the peace of God, which sur-passes all understanding, will guard your hearts and minds through Christ Jesus.
>
> Philippians 4:6-7

The peace of or from God is the peace that God gives us. It is the God kind of peace. It is the peace that comes from God. The peace of God is the kind of peace that God operates in. The peace of God will have you sleeping in a boat that is being severely tossed about in Hurricane Laura. The peace of God will have you leading the prisoners in praise and worship after your persecutors have beaten you and flogged you and thrown you in prison. The peace of God will have you playing dominoes with a hungry lion in the midst of a lion's den.

The Peace of or from God is by grace.

Peace like God

And third, as a result of what Christ did, we now have "peace like God." What do I mean by peace like God? In Romans, chapter twelve, verse eighteen, the Bible says, "If it is possible, as much as depends on you, live peaceably with all men." And in verse fourteen of Hebrews, chapter twelve, the Bible says, "Pursue peace with all people, and holiness, without which no one will see the Lord."

Peace like God is what causes you to respond in the same way that Christ responds. Peace like God is what you do. And peace like God is how you act. "As much as depends on you, live peaceably." That's what you do. "Pursue peace with all people." That's how you act.

Peace like God is by choice.

Since He is YHWH-Shalom, He has become your peace. You no longer have to worry, but you can let Him be your peace. You no longer have to lose sleep over that sort of thing because He is your peace. You no longer have to stress yourself out trying to figure out a solution because He is your peace. He is YHWH-Shalom, He is the Lord our Peace.

And because He is our Peace, God wants us to trust Him, and rest in Him, and rely on Him, and walk in the peace we have with Him, and the peace we have from Him, and the peace we have like Him.

> Therefore I say to you, do not worry about your life, what you will eat or what you will drink; nor about your body, what you will put on [...] Look at the birds of the air, for they neither sow nor reap nor gather into barns; yet your heavenly

#HeCompletesYou

Father feeds them. Are you not of more value than they? [...] So why do you worry about clothing? Consider the lilies of the field, how they grow: they neither toil nor spin; and yet I say to you that even Solomon in all his glory was not arrayed like one of these. Now if God so clothes the grass of the field, which today is, and tomorrow is thrown into the oven, will He not much more clothe you, O you of little faith? Therefore do not worry, saying, "What shall we eat?" or "What shall we drink?" or "What shall we wear?" For after all these things the Gentiles seek. For your heavenly Father knows that you need all these things. But seek first the kingdom of God and His righteousness, and all these things shall be added to you.

Matthew 6:25-33

He is *YHWH-Shalom*, the Lord our *Peace*. God wants you to know that He completes you, and God wants you to be confident in His love for you. You are to be free from fear and anxiety and worry, and rest in knowing that if God will take care of a little bird and dress a flower garden, surely He will take care of you and perfect everything that concerns you.

So Who is YHWH? YHWH is too big to contain. Who is YHWH? YHWH is too vast to describe. The best way to put it is that YHWH is whoever you need Him to be.

He is YHWH-Shalom. He is the Lord our Peace.

DR. MELVIN G. BARNEY, ESQ.

So when the devil tries to make you pace the floor at night worrying about your kids, you can say, "Not tonight, devil, the Lord's got my kids, and He is YHWH-Shalom, He is the Lord my Peace."

And when the devil tries to make you worry about what the outcome is going to be, you can say, "Not so, devil, God is working this thing together for my good, and He is YHWH-Shalom, He is the Lord my Peace."

And when the devil tries to make you have a nervous breakdown trying to figure out how to fix it, you can say, "It's not going to happen, devil, God's got the solution and the fix, and He is YHWH-Shalom, He is the Lord my Peace."

Jesus said, "After this manner pray, say, 'Hallowed be Your Name.'" If we want the manifestation of what the Name entails, we've got to hallow the Name. If we want the manifestation of what the Name promises, we have to hallow the Name. When we hallow the Name, we sow the Name. And the way we sow the Name is to speak the Name.

We thank You, oh God, that You are YHWH-Shalom. You are the Lord our Peace. And we thank you, oh God, that we don't have to succumb to the temptation to worry or be anxious about what's going to happen because You gave us an instruction.

You told us to be careful or anxious for nothing, but in everything by prayer and supplication, with thanksgiving, we are to let our request be made known to You, O God. So we thank You, YHWH-Shalom, for You have given us the prescription for peace. You told us to think about the things that are true, and honest, and just, and pure, and lovely, and of good report. You told us to search for the things that are of virtue and to seek out the things that are praiseworthy; you told us to focus our attention on those things.

#HeCompletesYou

We thank You that we have peace with You, O God. And we thank You that we have peace from You, O God. And Lord, we thank You that we have peace like You. You are YHWH-Shalom, You are the Lord our Peace.

CHAPTER 13

YHWH-SHAMMAH—THE LORD OUR FULLNESS

#BeGodInsideMinded

We have been examining the intersection between Exodus, chapter twenty, where God commands His people not to carry His Name in vain, and Luke, chapter eleven, where Jesus instructs us to "hallow" His Name. Let's go in the Bible, first to Exodus, chapter twenty, verse seven:

"You shall not take the Name of the LORD your God in vain, for the LORD will not hold him guiltless who takes His Name in vain" (Exodus 20:7).

Now let's look at the other foundation scripture, which comes from verse two of Luke, chapter eleven, where Jesus is speaking to His followers:

"He said to them, 'When you pray, say: Our Father in heaven, Hallowed be Your Name'" (Luke 11:2).

We have learned that when we hallow God's Name, we are sowing His Name, and to sow His Name is to hallow God's Name. The way we sow the Name is by speaking the Name. And because of the kingdom principle of sowing and reaping, we know that it is by speaking the Name that we usher in the power of God to manifest the promise, because God put the power in the Name to make itself come to pass. This is a kingdom principle. Jesus said, "The kingdom of God is as if a man should scatter seed on the ground."

When God talked to Moses, He told him, "I appeared to Abraham, Isaac, and Jacob by My title, El-Shaddai, because my relationship with them was limited, it was merely 'religious.' With them, it was about ritual. With them, it was about ceremony. With them, it was about formality. With them, it was about pomp and circumstance."

But God says, "As for you, I had more in mind. I do not merely want a 'religious' relationship with you, where we communicate every now and then, or every once in a while, or whenever there is a problem, or whenever there is an issue. That's a 'religious relationship.'" God says, "That's boring to Me." God says, "What I want for you is different. What I want for you is a personal relationship."

God wants us to spend some quality time with Him and make an effort to get to know Him. Let's not be too busy doing a whole bunch of whatever that we cannot make God a priority. Don't have so much going on that you have to put God on the back burner or maybe get to Him later if you can find the time. Bring God to the front of the line and make Him your priority. Don't settle for a religious relationship with God when you can have a personal relationship with Him.

Come on, let's get to know Him. God says, "Let Me introduce Myself to you. I am YHWH."

And when the devil tries to get you to believe that God does not hear you, you can tell him to shut up and call him out as a liar because you know your God. Or when the devil tries to tell you that sickness is the will of God for you, you can tell him to shut up and call him out as a liar because you know your God. Or when the devil tries to tell you that God wants you to be in lack, you can tell him to shut up and call him out as a liar because you know your God.

The Bible says that "the people who know their God shall be strong and carry out great exploits" (see Daniel 11:32). We need to know Him. He is YHWH.

We have also learned that YHWH is multi-faceted. You may be looking for Him to move one way, and He does something different. He can cause a bunch of knee bones to connect to a bunch of leg bones and emerge as a great army in a valley that is full of dry bones. He can take you from a place of bondage one day with absolutely nothing that you can call your own and bring you out of slavery the next day with the wealth of Egypt in hand. Now, all of a sudden, you are decked out in the best designer labels on your back and a bunch of jewels dangling from your head, and even your children bling out with a gang of gold hanging from their necks.

God can take the seed that you have sown during a time of famine and cause you to reap a hundredfold even in the midst of that famine, while people all around you are going under, because He is YHWH. That's why you cannot put Him in a box. That's why you cannot confine Him to do it your way. That's why you cannot instruct Him. You've got to let Him be Lord. He is YHWH! He is multi-faceted, like a diamond.

In this chapter, I want to explore another facet of YHWH, to Whom we will be introduced, in Ezekiel, chapter forty-eight and 1 John, chapter four:

> "And the name of the city from that day shall be: The Lord is There [*YHWH-Shammah*]" (Ezekiel 48:35).

#BeGodInsideMinded

"Greater is He that is in you, than he that is in the world" (see 1 John 4:4, KJV).

These scriptures speak of *YHWH-Shammah,* the Lord our *Fullness,* and the need for us to be God-inside-minded.

I was watching reruns of *Friends* on television the other day, and in this particular episode, Phoebe was involved in a conversation with Monica where she started chiding Monica, making jokes, and railing on Monica about her boyfriend, Chandler Bing. It was all in jest because Chandler was right in the next room, in earshot of the entire conversation. After a few rounds of this, Chandler Bing looked around the corner and said, "I'm right here." And they all started laughing. Now in that episode, Phoebe knew he was there all the time, which is partially why it was so funny. But even though she knew he was there, Phoebe was carrying on as though Chandler Bing was not present.

There are not too many times when you can get into a conversation about God where it does not come up that God is omniscient (all-knowing), is omnipotent (all-powerful), and omnipresent (all-present or everywhere). We talk as though we know He is right here with us. But even though we "know" that God is present, there are times that we act as though God has left the building and is nowhere to be found.

What I want to emphasize in this teaching is that He is YHWH-Shammah. God is right here. And not only is God right here, but God is right there. God is omnipresent. He is right here in the midst.

The Hebrew word *shammah* translates as "there," "here," "in the midst," "about us," "on every side," "in the circuit." God is present.

I want us to internalize the fact that God is in us. I want you to internalize the fact that God is inside you. I want you to become God-inside-minded.

It is important for us to understand that God is with us. But even though God is with us, He not just with us. I want us to understand that God is also among us. But even though God is among us, He is not just among us. I want us to understand that God is right here, in our midst. But even though God is right here, in our midst, He is not just in our midst. If you are born again, God is inside you. If you are born again, if you are saved, if you are blood-bought, if you have accepted Jesus Christ as your Lord and as your Savior, God lives inside you. We need to become God-inside-minded.

As we are studying the Name, YHWH, hopefully, it is becoming more and more clear that God desires an intimate relationship with His people. And as we follow the chronology from the beginning, in Genesis, down through time to today, and even beyond, to what the Bible prepares us to expect at the end time in the book of Revelation, the common thread is that our God is a relational God, Who has always wanted to dwell in the midst of His people.

Somebody might ask, "If that is the case, what happened?" And the answer is this: sin happened. Adam's sin caused the great schism and the great breach that separated us from God and that got us kicked out of God's presence, and that messed up the relationship that God intended for us to have with Him.

But even though Adam messed it up, it has been God's agenda all along to dwell in the midst of His people, and one thing we've learned about God is that He is the same yesterday, today, and forever. He does not change.

We find throughout the entire Bible, from Genesis to Revelation, an account of all God has done to reconnect with

#BeGodInsideMinded

His people and to dwell in the midst of His people because *God's agenda has always been to dwell in the midst of His people.*

Let's look at the chronology of God's agenda, which we assert, has always been to dwell in the midst of His people.

God in the Midst of His People in Eden

God's agenda has always been to dwell in the midst of His people. As we saw through God's interaction with Adam during the first few chapters of Genesis, God's desire was to dwell in the midst of His people in Eden. God enjoyed hanging out with Adam and fellowshipping with Adam from the start.

> And out of the ground the Lord God formed every beast of the field, and every fowl of the air; and brought them unto Adam to see what he would call them: and whatsoever Adam called every living creature, that was the name thereof.
>
> Genesis 2:19

God in the Midst of His People in the Wilderness

God's agenda has always been to dwell in the midst of His people. As we saw in studying the Pentateuch, when the children of Israel were wandering in the wilderness from Egypt to Canaan, God's plan was to be in their midst.

> And let them make Me a sanctuary, that I may dwell among them [...] You shall put the mercy seat on top of the ark, and in the ark you shall put the Testimony

> that I will give you. And there I will meet
> with you, and I will speak with you from
> above the mercy seat...
>
> Exodus 25:8, 21-22

God in the Midst of His People as the Christ

God's agenda has always been to dwell in the midst of His people. God's desire to dwell in the midst of His people was manifested in Christ, as we saw in the New Testament when He embodied human flesh.

> In the beginning was the Word, and the
> Word was with God, and the Word was
> God. He was in the beginning with God.
> All things were made through Him, and
> without Him nothing was made that was
> made [...] And the Word became flesh
> and dwelt among us.
>
> John 1:1-3, 14

Now, God Is Dwelling Inside His People, in the Person of the Holy Spirit

God's agenda has always been to dwell in the midst of His people. Now, God's desire to dwell in the midst of His people has been manifested since the day of Pentecost, in the Person of the Holy Spirit, Who came down to dwell inside of us.

> Or do you not know that your body is
> the temple of the Holy Spirit *[W]ho is*
> in you, [W]hom you have from God,

#BeGodInsideMinded

> and you are not your own? For you were bought at a price; therefore glorify God in your body and in your spirit, which are God's.
>
> 1 Corinthians 6:19-20

For now, until He brings heaven to earth and sets up His kingdom here in our midst where we can interact with Him throughout eternity, God has fulfilled His desire to dwell in the midst of His people. He is YHWH-Shammah. He is the Lord our Fullness.

Since YHWH lives inside of us, since He has made our bodies His abode, since our bodies are His temple, should we not act like it?

> Do not be unequally yoked together with unbelievers. For what fellowship has righteousness with lawlessness? And what communion has light with darkness? And what accord has Christ with Belial? Or what part has a believer with an unbeliever? And what agreement has the temple of God with idols? For you are the temple of the living God. As God has said: "I will dwell in them and walk among them. I will be their God, and they shall be My people."
>
> 2 Corinthians 6:14-16

Our bodies are the temple of God. And since He lives on the inside of me, I need to be God-inside-minded. And since He lives on the inside of you, you ought to be God-inside-minded. Because if you are saved, if you are born again, the Holy Spirit moved in, and when He moved in, He brought the whole Godhead with Him.

The Bible says that it is God Who is at work on the inside of you, in order to will and to do, of His own good pleasure (see Philippians 2:13). That's God on the inside keeping you, enabling you, and empowering you to do His will.

And the Bible says it is Christ in you, the hope of glory (see Colossians 1:27), because God's will is to reveal to you what He conceals from the ungodly, namely, the riches of His glory.

And the Bible says that your body is the temple of the Holy Spirit and that you are not even your own (see 1 Corinthians 6:19-20), for you have been bought or ransomed.

Hallelujah, you are so important to God that He ransomed you. And since He did all that to live in you, the least you can do is love Him. You are so important to God that He paid the ultimate price for you. And since He did that to live in you, the least you can do is spend quality time with Him. God loves you so much that He went into the enemy's camp and redeemed you. And since He has done all of that in order to live in you, the least you can do is make it a priority to get to know Him.

We need to be God-inside-minded. God did not ransom you for a religious relationship. He wants a personal relationship with you. We need to be God-inside-minded.

God did not pay the ultimate price to get you to talk to Him only when you need Him to get you out of trouble. God wants an intimate relationship with you. We need to be God-inside-minded.

God did not redeem you with the intent to leave you estranged from Him. God wants to be "all up in your Kool-

#BeGodInsideMinded

Aid," and He wants you to be all up in His. We need to be God-inside-minded.

Take a moment and really internalize the fact that God lives inside you.

The First Epistle of John, chapter four, verse four says this: "greater is [H]e that is in you, than he that is in the world" (see 1 John 4:4). The Greater One lives inside *you*. The One Who created the heavens and the earth lives in *you*. The One Who is all-powerful and all-mighty lives inside *you*. The "I Am That I Am" lives inside *you*.

We need to be God-inside-minded because to be God-inside-minded is to be victory-minded. How can we ever lose with God on the inside? How can we ever fail with God living in here? How can we ever go under with God on board? God Almighty lives inside of us. And He is the Greater One. There is nobody stronger. There is none that can overpower Him. There is no one who can overthrow Him. And there is nobody who can withstand Him. He is the Greater One, and yet, He lives inside of *you*.

We need to be God-inside-minded. Well, what is He doing in there? That depends on what you allow. He will lead, guide, and direct you if you allow it. He will teach you all things, show you the right way, and bring you down the path to victory if you follow Him. He will reprove you when you need correction, sustain you in your weakness, and no matter what's going on, He will never leave you nor forsake you. That's Who lives on the inside of *you*.

We need to be God-inside-minded. Let's look at some more of Who He is to you. He is your Helper, your Comforter, your Paraclete, and He lives in *you*. He is your own personal Counselor, Advocate, and Intercessor, and He lives in *you*. He is your Strengthener when you feel weak, Your Sustainer when you feel overwhelmed, and He is your Standby, that's the Friend Who will stick closer than a brother. And He lives in *you*.

We need to be God-inside-minded, for greater is He that is in us than He that is in the world.

So Who is YHWH? YHWH is too much to comprehend. Who is YHWH? YHWH is too vast to contain. The best way to put it is that YHWH is whoever you need Him to be.

He is YHWH-Shammah, He is the Lord our Fullness. He is YHWH-Shammah, He is God inside you.

So when the devil tries to tell you that God has abandoned you and you are in this thing all by yourself, you can say, "Not so, devil, for my God dwells inside of me, and He has promised that He will never leave me nor forsake me."

And when the devil tries to tell you that you are going down and that this one is surely going to take you out, you can say, "Not so, devil, for the greater One dwells inside me, and not even you can pluck me out of His hands.

And when the devil tries to tell you, "You've crossed the line, and God is mad at you, and this time God will not get you out of this," you can say, "You are a liar, devil, for God is yet at work in me, and he walks with me, and he talks with me, and he tells me I'm His own…"

Jesus said, "After this manner pray, say, 'Hallowed be Your Name.'" If we want the manifestation of what the Name entails, we've got to hallow the Name. If we want the manifestation of what the Name promises, we have to hallow the Name. When we hallow the Name, we sow the Name. And the way we sow the Name is to speak the Name.

So we thank You, oh God, that You are YHWH-Shammah. You are the Lord our Fullness. And we thank You, Lord, that You are YHWH-Shammah. You are the God Who

#BeGodInsideMinded

lives on the inside of us. We give You praise, oh God, that You alone are the Greater One, and we know that greater is our God, Who is in us than he that is in the world.

And so we magnify You for giving us a direct link to You because You live in us. And we give You praise, O Lord, that we can be intimate with You because You live in us. And we glorify You, our God, that we can embrace You personally because You live in us.

Thank You, Lord, that our bodies are Your temple and that You dwell mightily on the inside of us. We thank You that because You live in us, we have power over the enemy. And we thank You that because You live in us, we get to rise above the things of this world, for You are the greater One Who lives in us, and You are greater than he that is in the world.

CHAPTER 14

YHWH-RAPHA—
THE LORD OUR HEALER

#FreeYourMindAndTheRestWillFollow

We have two passages of Scripture that we have been relying on for foundational purposes. The first is found in the twentieth chapter of Exodus, verse seven, and it reads: "You shall not take the Name of the LORD your God in vain, for the LORD will not hold him guiltless who takes His Name in vain" (Exodus 20:7).

The other foundation scripture comes from the Gospel according to St. Luke, chapter eleven and verse two, where Jesus is speaking to those of us who are His followers: "He said to them, 'When you pray, say: Our Father in heaven, Hallowed be Your Name'" (Luke 11:2).

Many of us who grew up in church can attest to the fact that we were taught to recite what they called "The Lord's Prayer" at an early age, but we really had no clue what was meant by the phrase, "hallowed be Your Name."

Our intent in this book has been to clear all of that up. We have taught that "to hallow" the Name of the Lord is to honor His Name, to sanctify or elevate His Name, to recognize His Name as holy, and mighty, and powerful. We have emphasized that the way we "hallow" or "sanctify" or "honor" God's Name is by embracing the fact that the power is in the Name. God's Name contains within itself the power to make itself come to pass.

We have also learned that when we hallow God's Name, we are sowing His Name. Additionally, we have emphasized that the way we sow the Name is by speaking the Name. And because of the kingdom principle of sowing and reaping, we know that it is by speaking the Name that we usher in the power of God to manifest the promise because God put the power in the Name to make itself come to pass. This is a kingdom principle. Jesus said Himself, "The kingdom of God is as if a man should scatter seed on the ground."

Even though it is clear that God desires a personal relationship with His people, it is a struggle for too many Christians. Too many are more comfortable with ritual, ceremony, formality, pomp, and circumstance than with spending time in His presence and getting to know Him. Nevertheless, we should not settle for a religious relationship with God when we can have a personal relationship with Him.

It pays to know Him.

When you know Him, the devil can't make you believe that all that trouble that has tried to overtake you is from God. Because you know Him.

And when you know Him, the devil can't make you believe that it was God Who caused you to suffer those losses and experience that need. Because you know Him.

And when you know Him, the devil can't make you believe that the sickness and disease that has plagued you is the will of God. Because you know Him.

The Bible says that "the people who know their God shall be strong and carry out great exploits" (see Daniel 11:32). Saints, we've got to know Him. He is YHWH.

And we have learned that YHWH is a multi-faceted God Who, like a diamond, has many dimensions and many angles. That's why God couldn't even answer Moses's question when he asked, "Who are You?" God could only say, "You want to know how to describe Me? I Am That I Am." You have it fixed in your mind that God is going to do one thing, and He does a whole different thing. You are looking for God to move one way, and He comes a whole different way. You expect Him to lay hands on the blinded eyes, and instead, He smears clay balls made of spit on them and causes the person to come forth seeing. You expect Him to have compassion for a woman who pleads with Him to deliver her daughter, and instead, He ignores her, calls her a dog but later on commends her for having the faith that causes her daughter to be healed. You expect Him to get to His sick friend in time to keep him from dying, and instead, He waits until the friend dies so He can raise him from the dead.

That's why you cannot try to box Him in. That's why you cannot try to get Him to do it your way. That's why you cannot counsel or instruct Him. You've got to let Him be Lord. He is YHWH!

And for this next facet that I want to talk about, we will need to go to Exodus, chapter fifteen, verse twenty-six.

> And [YHWH] said, "If you diligently
> heed the voice of the Lord your God
> and do what is right in His sight, give
> ear to His commandments and keep all
> His statutes, I will put none of the dis-
> eases on you which I have brought on

#FreeYourMindAndTheRestWillFollow

the Egyptians. For I am the Lord [W]ho heals you [*YHWH-Rapha*]."

Exodus 15:26, modified

The focus of this chapter is the Name, *YHWH-Rapha*, the Lord our *Healer*.

In 1992, the sensational female group, En Vogue, released a smash hit called "Free Your Mind," in which they address how a person's erroneous thoughts and twisted beliefs and prejudiced convictions and preconceived notions can be costly and cause the person to miss opportunities. In the song's hook, En Vogue, also known as "The Funky Divas," tells the person to "Free your mind, and the rest will follow." In "Free Your Mind," they identify the person's thinking as the root of the person's problems.

God has given His people a Book of Promises. This book is full of exceeding, great, and precious promises (see 2 Peter 1:4), one of which is physical healing. While on earth, Jesus went about healing every sickness and every disease (see Matthew 8:16-17), making it clear that it is God's will for everyone to be free from sickness and disease. God ratified His promises through a covenant, in which He poured out His own blood, as a testament of His integrity. Yet, notwithstanding all of this evidence of God's will, there are hosts of people in the Body of Christ who love God with all their hearts but struggle with the question of whether healing belongs to them.

They have seen the promise of healing in the Word, but because they are confronting a number of symptoms, they tell themselves that God has not healed them. They have studied the Scriptures, but since it has been such a long time, they have convinced themselves that healing is not God's will for them. They know what the Word says about healing, but they listen to messages across the pulpit from preachers who tell them that God does not heal anymore and that they are suffering for the glory of God.

And as a result, like the people who En Vogue are confronting in that song, many of God's people are filled with erroneous thoughts, twisted beliefs, prejudiced convictions, and preconceived notions that are robbing them of the healings that God has promised them.

But as En Vogue said, you've got to free your mind, and the rest will follow. Likewise, if you are a born-again believer, you've got to embrace the promises of God. You've got to stand on the Word of God. You've got to reject anything that refutes the Word of God. You've got to free your mind of anything that goes contrary to the Word of God.

Sickness and Disease Are Not the Will of God for His People

The starting point that we need to establish for this teaching is that sickness and disease are not the will of God for His people. If you are a child of God and you are afflicted in your body, you need to understand and embrace the fact that the affliction that plagues you is not God's will for you. I understand that many of God's people are suffering from a number of horrible physical assaults, but we need to know that contrary to any lie the devil has told you: first, sickness and disease are not the will of God for you; and second, God is not the source of it.

One of the snares that the enemy uses to keep you bound and from receiving from God is that he talks to you; he puts thoughts in your mind and tries to persuade you that God does not want you healed. He wants you to believe that it is God's will for you to be in that state, and that God is mad at you, and that God is the One Who afflicted you,

#FreeYourMindAndTheRestWillFollow

and that God is somehow getting glory from you being in that dilapidated state. But the devil is a liar. If you want your healing, you have got to free your mind so that the rest can follow. You've got to rebuke those thoughts and take authority over those lies and bind that confusion. You've got to recognize the lie of the enemy, and you've got to know that he is waging war in your mind.

The Bible says it this way, in 2 Corinthians, chapter ten, beginning from verse three:

> For though we walk in the flesh, we do not war according to the flesh. For the weapons of our warfare are not carnal but mighty in God for pulling down strongholds, casting down arguments and every high thing that exalts itself against the knowledge of God, bringing every thought into captivity to the obedience of Christ.
>
> 2 Corinthians 10:3-5

If you have been conditioned to believe that God wants you sick, you need to free your mind so the rest can follow.

If you have somehow accepted as the fact that you are going to just have to take that sickness and disease with you to the grave, you need to free your mind so the rest can follow.

If you have been confused or discouraged about whether God is ever going to heal you or whether it's God's will to heal you, you need to free your mind so the rest can follow.

You need to free your mind, because the battle is in the mind.

This scripture says our battles are not against flesh and blood. If you are a believer, stop fussing and fighting with people. Let God handle them. Your battles, according to the Word of God, are spiritual battles. Everything else is just a distraction. The Bible says your battle is in your own mind.

There are strongholds in your mind, in which the devil has you tied up and entangled. And the Bible says these strongholds are the reasonings, the arguments, the thoughts you think, which cause you to question God. That's where your battle is. The doubt. The unbelief. The confusion.

This scripture tells us if it contradicts the Word of God, you've got to fight against it. This scripture tells us if it is out of alignment with the Word of God, you've got to reject it. This scripture tells us if it questions the integrity of God's Word, you've got to cast it down. And with respect to our healing, it is the devil, not God, who wants to block your healing. God says, "I am YHWH-Rapha; I am the God Who heals you."

So, let me say it again: sickness and disease are not the will of God for His people. Think about it: from the beginning, when God created mankind, sickness and disease were not in the mix. When God created Adam and set him in the Garden of Eden, he was free of sickness and disease, and the intent was that he would live forever. Sickness and disease were not a part of God's plan from the beginning.

However, Adam's state of wholeness was contingent on his obedience, just like yours and mine are. And just like Adam, it is in our disobedience that we open the doors for the enemy to attack us.

> And the Lord God commanded the man, saying, "Of every tree of the garden you may freely eat; but of the tree of the knowledge of good and evil you shall not

#FreeYourMindAndTheRestWillFollow

eat, for in the day that you eat of it you
shall surely die."

Genesis 2:16-17

Healing: the Bad, the Good, the Issue

The bad: sickness, disease, pain, death, are all consequences of Adam's disobedience.

It was Adam's sin that opened up the floodgates to sickness and disease. When Adam sinned, he was cursed, his body was cursed, his offspring was cursed, and the process of physical decay set in.

Thus, *the bad* is that sickness, disease, pain, death—are all consequences of Adam's disobedience.

The good: Christ suffered the penalty for our sickness and disease, and Christ paid the price for our deliverance.

Nevertheless, sickness and suffering *have never been* the will of God for His people. Pain and disease *have never been* in the plan of God for His people.

Thus, *the good* is this: God fixed it Himself. That's one of the reasons Christ came. Adam got us into a mess that he could not get us out of, so Christ Himself suffered the penalty for our sickness and disease, and Christ Himself paid the price for our deliverance.

"But He was wounded for our transgressions, He was bruised for our iniquities; The chastisement for our peace was upon Him, And by His stripes we are healed" (Isaiah 53:5).

DR. MELVIN G. BARNEY, ESQ.

The issue: we've got to free our minds so the rest can follow. We've got to believe.

Therefore, we must resolve within ourselves that the debt has been paid, that Christ handled it, and that healing belongs to us. So then, if Christ has already handled it, what is *the issue?* If Christ has already handled it, why are the saints still inflicted with sickness and disease? Because we've got to believe it. We've got to embrace it. We've got to accept it by faith.

The same faith it takes to receive salvation is the kind of faith it takes to receive your healing. Just like we took God at His Word that we were saved before we stopped cutting up, and we took God at His Word that we were saved before we felt saved, we have to take God at His Word that we are healed before the pain stops cutting up, and we have to take God at His Word that we have been healed, even before our body feels healed. *We've got to free our minds so the rest can follow.* Because it is with the same measure you mete that it shall be measured back to you.

In Mark, chapter four, verse twenty-four, Jesus said, "Take heed what you hear. With the same measure you use [mete, KJV], it will be measured to you; and to you who hear, more will be given" (Mark 4:24).

The issue is "the measure with which you mete." In other words, what do you believe? He said that it is with the same measure you mete that it shall be measured back to you. If you believe and internalize what God says, that's what you will get. If, instead, you reject what God says and believe what the doctor says, then *that's* what you will get. Or, if the physical symptoms cause you to reject what God says, then *that* is what you will get. It is with the same measure you mete that it shall be measured back to you.

#FreeYourMindAndTheRestWillFollow

Therefore, the issue is, you've got to free your minds so the rest can follow. The issue is as long as the devil can make you doubt the Word of God, he can block your healing. The issue is as long as the devil can make you think God has not done it yet for you, he can block your healing. The issue is as long as the devil can make you believe you are still waiting on God to move on your behalf, he can block your healing.

But we receive everything we get from God by faith. The same way you got saved is the way you get healed. You got saved by believing that you were saved because the Word said if you confess certain things and believe certain things, you would be saved (see Romans 10:9). You did not get saved by believing that someday in the future, you would be saved. Once you confessed those things that the Word said to confess and believed those things that the Word said to believe, you knew you were saved. Why? Because you believed God's Word.

Today, you know you are saved in spite of anything to the contrary. You know you are saved in spite of how you feel. You know you are saved, even if you slip and do some things that don't look saved. Why? Because you believe God's Word. You got saved by believing that you were saved because you believed God's Word. And since God put the power in the Word to make itself come to pass…

Likewise, you get healed by believing that you *were* healed because the Word says that you *were* healed. You have to know you have been healed in spite of anything to the contrary. You have to know that you have been healed, even when your body does not feel healed. You have to know that you have been healed, even when the symptoms in your body suggest that you are not healed. Why? Because you believe God's Word. Let's look at what He says in the second chapter of 1 Peter: "[W]ho Himself bore our sins in His own body on the tree, that we, having died to sins, might live for righ-teousness—by whose stripes you were healed" (1 Peter 2:24).

This scripture says you "*were*" healed. He did not say, "You will be healed." He said, "You *were* healed." That is past tense. That means it is done. That means it is concluded. That means it has already happened. That means there is nothing else for God to do... Therefore, healing is not a result of believing that you will be healed. Healing is a result of believing that you "*were*" healed, even before the healing manifests in your body. And we've got to free our minds so the rest can follow. It's by believing what the Bible says, that "by His stripes, we were healed" even before our bodies feel healed that we get healed. In other words, we've got to call those things which be not as though they were.

We've got to believe God when He says He sent His Word and healed them and delivered them from their destructions (see Psalm 107:20).

We've got to trust God when He tells us to bless the Lord and forget not all His benefits: because He forgives all our iniquities, and He heals all our diseases (see Psalm 103:2-3).

We've got to obey God when He instructs us to attend to His Words and incline our ears to His sayings. And to not let them depart from our eyes, but to keep them in the midst of our hearts. Because He promised us that His Words would be life to those of us who find them and health to all our flesh (see Proverbs 4:20-22).

And how is that possible? Because God put the power in the Word to make itself come to pass. And if we free our minds, then the rest will follow. So as long as we sow the Word in the good ground of our hearts, it shall come to pass. Why? Because it is a kingdom principle, and God put the power in the Word to make itself come to pass.

#FreeYourMindAndTheRestWillFollow

So Who is YHWH? YHWH is too much to wrap your mind around.

Who is YHWH? YHWH is too complicated to try to explain.

The best way to put it is that YHWH is the "I Am That I Am." YHWH is whoever you need Him to be. He is YHWH-Rapha, He is the Lord our Healer. He is YHWH-Rapha, He is the God that heals you.

So when the devil tries to tell you that God wants you sick and diseased, you can say, "That's a lie, devil, for the Bible says that my God forgives all my iniquities and heals all my diseases."

And when the devil tries to tell you that God put that illness on you in order to teach to something, you can say, "Not so, devil, for He Himself took my sickness and He Himself bare my diseases."

And when the devil tries to suggest that if God wanted you healed, He would have healed you by now, you can say, "Get behind me, devil, for He was wounded for my transgression, and He was bruised for my iniquities: and the chastisement of my peace was upon Him, and with His stripes, I am healed."

Jesus said, "After this manner pray, say, 'Hallowed be Your Name.'" If we want the manifestation of what the Name entails, we've got to hallow the Name. If we want the manifestation of what the Name promises, we have to hallow the Name. When we hallow the Name, we sow the Name. And the way we sow the Name is to speak the Name.

So we thank You, oh God, that You are YHWH-Rapha. You are the Lord our Healer. And we thank You, Lord, that You are YHWH-Rapha. You are the God Who *heals* us. And I give You praise, O God, that You have caused us to free our minds of the doubt and unbelief. And I magnify you, God, for letting us know that You are not a man that you can lie and that you are not the son of man that you can repent.

Thank You, Lord, that You were wounded for our transgressions and bruised for our iniquities. Thank you, God, that the chastisement for our peace was laid upon You and that on account of Your stripes, we are healed. I thank you that because Your Word is at work on the inside of us, we can reject sickness and stand against disease; and You said, if we resist the devil, He will flee from us. Therefore, anything and everything that is going on in our bodies that are not like You, has got to go from our bodies. In Jesus's Name. You are *YHWH-Rapha*, the Lord our *Healer*.

CHAPTER 15

YHWH-YIREH—THE LORD OUR PROVIDER

#GodWillTestYouToBlessYou

Exodus, chapter twenty, verse seven, reads as follows: "You shall not take the Name of the LORD your God in vain, for the LORD will not hold him guiltless who takes His Name in vain" (Exodus 20:7).

And in Luke, chapter eleven and verse two, Jesus gives us the model for prayer: "He said to them, 'When you pray, say: Our Father in heaven, Hallowed be Your Name'" (Luke11:2).

From chapter to chapter, we have been exploring in great detail what the Word of God means when we are told not to take the Name of the Lord our God in vain. We have been in an exhaustive study of what it actually looks like to "hallow" or "sanctify" the Lord's Name. And God is revealing to us, as we continue to dig into this teaching, that there is a correlation between the instruction not to take the Name of the Lord in vain, and Jesus's teaching that we are to deliberately and intentionally "hallow the Name" of the Lord.

Instead of taking God's Name in vain, we are being directed to carry His Name with purpose.

We do so when we embrace and tap into the power that is in the Name. We are learning that when we hallow God's Name, we are sowing His Name as a seed. And we have emphasized that the way we sow the Name is by speaking the Name. Because of the kingdom principle of sowing and reaping, we know that it is by speaking the Name that we usher in the power of God to manifest the promise, because God put the power in the Word to make itself come to pass. This is a kingdom principle. Jesus Christ said, "So is the kingdom of God: it is as if a man should scatter seed on the ground."

One of the goals of this book is to drive into our spirits what a resource we have available in the Name of the Lord, in hopes of inspiring and motivating us to use and rely on His Name as such. And in the course of this study, we have noted that there is a distinction between a *title* and a *name*.

The titles of God tell us what He does, so they reinforce for us that we can trust Him because God is always going to do what He does. You can take that to the bank. Nevertheless, we are yet being challenged to understand that God wants more of a relationship with us than a title can offer. Merely knowing God by His titles limits us to a "religious" relationship with Him; that's where we would only communicate with God when we need Him to do something. That's where we only come to Him when we are in trouble. That's where serving Him is somewhat a "chore" or a "got to." "Got to" go to church. "Got to" pray. "Got to" pay tithes. "Got to" obey His Word. That's religion, and Jesus came to set us free from religion.

God did not save us for religion. You can have that with Buddha and Muhammad and Hari Krishna. God saved us for relationship. When we talk about relationship, it is no longer "got to," it is "get to." We "get to" be His children.

We "get to" fellowship with Him and hang out with Him. We "get to" sow tithe and offering seed that He is going to multiple back to us. We "get to" partake of His blessings and His miracles and His covenant. We "get to" access Him and spend time with Him and know Him.

God does not want religion from us. God wants a personal relationship with us. He wants an intimate connection with us. God doesn't just want you to know about Him. God wants you to know Him.

And when you know YHWH, the devil can't make you feel like you are missing out on a bunch of fun by serving God. Because you know YHWH.

And when you know YHWH, the devil can't make you believe that it costs you something to obey God. Because you know YHWH.

And when you know YHWH, the devil can't make you believe that you've got to settle for less than what God has promised you. Because you know YHWH.

The Scripture says that "the people who know their God shall be strong and carry out great exploits" (see Daniel 11:32). It pays to know Him. He is YHWH.

And YHWH is a multi-faceted God with many dimensions and many angles. He describes Himself as the "I Am That I Am." Somebody may want to know, 'I Am what?' 'I Am unpredictable.'"

You might be looking for God to come one way, but instead, He comes another. You might be expecting God to respond according to a certain pattern, but instead, He nixes that pattern and does something totally different.

You expect Him to provide resources for you through your job, but instead, he sends you fishing, and the snapper you hook has the money in its mouth.

#GodWillTestYouToBlessYou

You expect Him to use the mighty warriors in the land to combat the enemy, but instead, He uses a little boy with a slingshot to bring down Goliath.

You expect God to keep them from throwing you in the burning fiery furnace, but instead, He gets in the fire with you and makes sure you don't get burned.

That's why you cannot try to box Him in. That's why you cannot try to get Him to do it your way. That's why you cannot counsel or instruct Him. You've got to let Him be Lord. He is YHWH!

YHWH is multi-faceted, like a diamond. And for this next facet of YHWH that we are going to introduce, we will need to go to the twenty-second chapter of Genesis, and though I am tempted to talk about the entire chapter, I am going to restrain myself and address only verses twelve through fourteen.

> And [the Lord] said, "Do not lay your hand on the lad, or do anything to him; for now I know that you fear God, since you have not withheld your son, your only son, from Me." Then Abraham lifted his eyes and looked, and there behind him was a ram caught in a thicket by its horns. So Abraham went and took the ram, and offered it up for a burnt offering instead of his son. And Abraham called the name of the place, [*YHWH-Yireh,* lit. the Lord *reveals*]; as it is said to this day, "In the Mount of the Lord it shall be [revealed/seen]."
>
> Genesis 22:12-14

The subject of this chapter is the Name *YHWH-Yireh*, the Lord our *Provider*.

Anyone who has struggled economically for an extended period of time can attest that one of the most challenging barriers to overcome, even for the blood-bought, blood-washed child of God, even for one who is saved, sanctified, and filled with the precious Holy Ghost, even for one who loves God with all her heart, with all her soul, with all her mind, and with all of her strength is the roadblock that the enemy throws in our faces to cause us to question whether prosperity is the will of God for us.

Now I am not talking about somebody who just had a brief stint during a brief stretch of time where he might have fallen behind in a bill or two. I am talking about 'sho nuf poverty. I am talking about generational poverty. I am talking about the kind that feels like bondage. I am talking about the kind that feels like a curse. I am talking about the kind that feels like, no matter what you do, you can't break free of it.

When you have been in that state, and when that is all you know, and when you have tried everything you know, and when you have come to terms with it, and when you have learned to be content therein, it is a challenge to believe that God wants you in abundance. You can see it for everybody else. You can see the power of God move on behalf of others. You can rejoice with others who rejoice and celebrate with others who get their breakthrough, but when it comes to you... Many have resigned in their hearts that "this is my lot in life, and I am okay."

I would liken it to the widow woman of Zarephath who said, "I have one cup of cornmeal left, and my plan is to make one little hoecake of cornbread with it, and I am going to share it with my child as our last meal before we die" (see 1 Kings 17:10-12).

#GodWillTestYouToBlessYou

But the prophet messed up her theology on that day. And just like the prophet blew her away on that day, I am here at this time to mess up somebody's theology, wreck somebody's foundation, and stir up some things that you don't want me to bother.

Poverty, lack, insufficiency, want, struggle, going without, doing without, having to "rob Peter to pay Paul," and living from paycheck to paycheck are not the will of God for His people.

In the last chapter, we talked about one of the devices that the enemy uses to ensnare the people of God. In order to keep us bound and from receiving from God, the devil talks to us; he puts thoughts in our minds. He tries to convince you that God does not want you in abundance. He tries to get you to think that God's will for you is to be in lack. The devil wants you to believe that if it was God's will for you to prosper, you would have it already. He wants you to believe that God is not concerned about your financial well-being.

But that devil is a liar, and like we said last time, if you want to come out of this rut, you have got to free your mind so that the rest can follow. You've got to rebuke those thoughts and take authority over those lies and bind that confusion. You've got to recognize the lie of the enemy, and you've got to know that he is waging war in your mind. And you've got to know that it is God's will for you to prosper.

The devil wants you bound, but according to the Third Epistle of John, verse two, not only does God want you to be in good health, but God's will for you is to prosper in direct proportion to how your soul prospers.

That being said, if I find myself in perpetual financial struggle, this is telling me what I can do about it. I need to look into my soul; in other words, I need to check into what I am thinking. What do I believe? Do I believe what God says, or do I believe what the devil says? You've got to free your mind, because with whatever measure you mete, it shall be measured unto you.

God has given us the recipe for coming out of debt. God has given us the way to get free of lack. God has given us the roadmap to be delivered from financial bondage, and that is the kingdom principle of sowing and reaping.

Remember how Jesus summed it up in Mark, chapter four? Jesus was saying, "It would behoove you to know this parable." He was saying, "It would be to your advantage to understand what I am talking about here." He was saying, "If you don't get anything else I've said to you, get this…" Jesus revealed that the kingdom of God operates on the principle of sowing and reaping.

Let's go to Mark, chapter four.

> "Listen! Behold, a sower went out to sow [...] But other seed fell on good ground and yielded a crop that sprang up, increased and produced: some thirtyfold, some sixty, and some a hundred."
> [...] And He said to them, "Do you not understand this parable? How then will you understand all the parables? The sower sows the word."
>
> Mark 4:3, 8, 13-14

Because of what Jesus said here, I call this "the granddaddy parable." Jesus suggests that there is nothing more important than this. This here will unlock the resources of heaven for you if you don't miss it. What is He talking about?

Here, Jesus speaking to a great multitude, a captive audience, has their full attention, could have talked about

#GodWillTestYouToBlessYou

anything—but starts talking about seed. In verse three, He says, "A sower went out to sow."

And He gives this account, which they could all relate to. They all knew about farming and how sowing seed works. But He describes this as a parable, which means it has a spiritual significance that could be a tremendous blessing to those who want to hear. Though they understood the principle of sowing seed and reaping a harvest from the seed that you sow, what they may not have known is that this is a spiritual law. This is a universal law. In order to reap a harvest, you've got to sow seed. And as long as you sow seed, you will reap a harvest.

Whether they made the spiritual connection or not, anybody who knows anything about seeds knows that there are *two failproof things about the seed.*

The first is this: the seed that is not sown will never reap a harvest.

This is a spiritual law. This is a universal law. In order to reap a harvest, you've got to sow the seed. If you have a bag of seeds and you leave it sitting on your windowsill, I don't care how much you fast. I don't care how faithful you are in church attendance. I don't care how much you love God: if you don't sow the seed, it will never reap a harvest.

God's desire is for you to prosper. God's will is for you to be blessed. God's heart is for you to always have more than enough. And God has provided the roadmap to your prosperity, which is in the kingdom principle of sowing and reaping. Jesus said, "So is the kingdom of God as if a man should scatter seed on the ground." Saints, we've got to sow seed.

The second failproof thing about the seed is this: the seed that is sown in good ground will always reap a harvest.

This is a spiritual law. This is a universal law. A seed that is sown in good ground does not discriminate. It will always reap a harvest. If you sow it in good ground, if you keep the bugs out, if you don't let the birds get to it, if you keep it well watered, if you keep the weeds out, if you take care of it, that seed is going to reap a harvest, and the devil cannot stop it. Why? Because it is a kingdom principle.

The thing about the seed is that a seed that is sown does not care who you are: if you plant it, it will grow. The seed that is sown does not worry about your background. If you plant it, it will grow. The seed that is sown does not concern itself with your pedigree, or whether your father left before you were three years old, or whether your mother neglected you while she was strung out on drugs. If you plant it, it will grow.

Why? Because the entire kingdom of God operates on the concept of seed that is sown. This is the crux of the kingdom of God. This is the kingdom principle. Jesus said, "So is the kingdom of God as if a man should sow seed in the ground."

And when we go over to Malachi, chapter three, verse ten, God really brings this point home.

> "Bring all the tithes into the storehouse, that there may be food in My house, and try Me now in this," says the Lord of hosts, "If I will not open for you the windows of heaven and pour out for you such blessing that there will not be room enough to receive it."
>
> Malachi 3:10

Now, like many of you, I grew up in church, and like many of you, I have heard this scripture in church all of my life. But when I have heard it, the focus has generally been on

#GodWillTestYouToBlessYou

171

the part we did not read, about the people robbing God. And though I do believe we are stealing from God when we don't tithe, that is not what I want to focus on. And when I have heard it, the focus has generally been on the part we did not read, about being cursed when you don't tithe. And though I believe we do bring a curse upon ourselves by stealing from God, that's not what I want to focus on. And when I have heard it, the focus has generally been on the part about how we can get back into good with God if we just go ahead and bring Him His tithe. And though I believe we can get the curse off of our backs by tithing, that's not what I want to focus on.

What I want to focus on right here right now is the revelation that God gave me regarding verse ten, which substantiates the kingdom principle of sowing and reaping.

When we look at Malachi, chapter three, verse ten, the part that says God will open up the windows of heaven and "pour out for you such blessing that there will not be room enough to receive it" makes perfect sense if you understand how seed works and if you are looking at this through the kingdom principle of sowing and reaping.

Remember, theirs was an agrarian culture. For them, wealth was accumulated by what crops they grew and what livestock they raised. With respect to one's crops, whether I own one acre of land, or one thousand acres of land, or one million acres of land—no matter what—even if I start with just a few apple seeds, because of this kingdom principle of sowing and reaping, as long as I plant my seed, I am going to reap apple trees. And if I keep on sowing the seed, no matter how hard the devil tries, he cannot stop me from reaping what I have sown, because God put the power in the seed to make itself come to pass.

Therefore, at some point, whether I am on one acre of land, or one thousand acres of land, or one million acres of land, I am going to run out of space, and my harvest will be bigger than the room I have to receive. Why? Because seed that is sown in good ground will always reap a harvest. And God put the power in the seed to make itself come to pass. This is a kingdom principle.

God has given us the recipe for coming out of debt. God has given us the way to get free of lack. God has given us the roadmap to be delivered from financial bondage, and that is the kingdom principle of sowing and reaping. Thus, if you are struggling in your finances, the question for you is, what are you doing with your seed?

It is important to note that God does not promise to give everybody a whole bunch of stuff. However, God does promise to give everybody some seed, and if you do what you are supposed to do with your seed, you can accumulate a whole bunch of stuff.

That's why you can have some people who inherit great wealth and others who go from rags to riches. If you know what to do with your seed, you can accumulate a whole bunch of stuff. Either way, it is with what measure you mete that it shall be measured to you. For some, your income from your job is your seed. For some, your retirement is your seed. For some, your investments are your seed. For some, your social security is your seed. And for some, even your welfare check can be your seed. But if you do what you are supposed to do with your seed, you can accumulate a whole bunch of stuff. Why? Because it is a kingdom principle. And God put the power in the seed to make itself come to pass.

Once again, the question is, what are you doing with your seed? You don't have to beg anybody for anything. Just do what you are supposed to do with your seed. You don't have to worry about how you are going to make it until the next time you get paid. Just do what you are supposed to do with your seed. You don't have to concern yourself with the fact that it looks like everybody around you is blossoming except you. Just do what you are supposed to do with your seed.

And what is it that you are supposed to do with the seed? You are supposed to sow it. It is a kingdom principle. And God put the power in the seed to make itself come to pass.

When we come back over to Abraham, in the twenty-second chapter of Genesis, if we were to back up some in that chapter, we would find that God had given him a challenge and that God had given him a test. Shameless plug: I taught a message from this passage before called, "God Will Test You in Order to Bless You." You need to get that message.

The Bible says that after God had brought Abraham out of Ur of the Chaldeans where he was an idolater, and after God had made a covenant with him, and after God had fought battle after battle after battle for him, and after God had multiplied him exceedingly, and after God had finally given him Isaac, the son of promise, God had the unmitigated gall to test Abraham with that son. Saints, God will test you, but it's only because He intends to bless you.

Here, the Bible says that God tested Abraham. And the Scripture says in verse two that God said to Abraham, "Take now your son, your only son Isaac, whom you love, and go to the land of Moriah, and offer him there as a burnt offering on one of the mountains of which I shall tell you" (Genesis 22:2).

"Do what? Offer him as a burnt offering? God, you mean like you do with tithes and bulls and rams when you sacrifice them on the altar? You mean like you do with offerings and goats and turtle doves when you sacrifice them on the altar? Are you kidding me? Did Abraham hear that correctly?" Yes, he did, because if you look back up at verse one, the Bible told us that this was a test.

What was God testing? God was testing his faith. His obedience. Whether he loved God with all his heart. Whether he loved Isaac more than he loved God. There is an assortment of things that God could have been testing. And just like with Abraham, there is an assortment of things that God will test with you. God wants us to love Him with all of our hearts. God wants us to place no other gods in His place. God wants us to obey Him at any cost. Any of that is fodder for God to test. There is an assortment of things that God will test, but, saints of God, you had better believe it when I tell you that God will test you from time to time.

The test may be, "What do you have in your possession that you are not willing to give up for Me?" Or the test may be, "What is so precious or important to you that you cannot give it up for Me?" Or the test may be, "How much do you really trust Me to do what I said I would do?" Or the test may be, "Do you really believe My Word, or do you fear I might not come through for you?"

God says, "I am YHWH-Yireh, I Am your Provider. Now, do you believe Me? I am YHWH-Yireh, I Am your Provider. Now, do you trust Me?" God will test you.

And when we follow Abraham down in this passage of Scripture, we see that He truly trusted God. When we follow Abraham in this passage of Scripture, we see that He believed God. When we follow Abraham in this passage of Scripture, we see that He obeyed God. When we follow Abraham in this passage of Scripture, we see that He was willing to give what was most important to him over to God. And because he passed the test, that's when God showed up.

#GodWillTestYouToBlessYou

Let's pick up at verse nine.

> Then they came to the place of which God had told him. And Abraham built an altar there and placed the wood in order; and he bound Isaac his son and laid him on the altar, upon the wood. And Abraham stretched out his hand and took the knife to slay his son. But the Angel of the Lord called to him from heaven and said, "Abraham, Abraham!" So he said, "Here I am." And He said, "Do not lay your hand on the lad, or do anything to him; for now I know that you fear God, since you have not withheld your son, your only son, from Me." Then Abraham lifted his eyes and looked, and there behind him was a ram caught in a thicket by its horns. So Abraham went and took the ram, and offered it up for a burnt offering instead of his son. And Abraham called the name of the place, The-Lord-Will-Provide [*YHWH-Yireh*]; as it is said to this day, "In the Mount of the Lord it shall be [seen]."
>
> Genesis 22:9-14

Now in most of our Bibles, this is translated as "the Lord will provide," and in many of our Bibles, it says, "in the Mount of the Lord it shall be provided." And I get that, and I am okay with that. But in spite of all of that, I think it is important to note that the actual Hebrew renders it as

YHWH-Yireh, which in Hebrew means, "The Lord reveals or causes it to be seen."

The reason I bring this up is because when we look at the Scripture, it says in verse thirteen that "Abraham lifted his eyes and looked, and there behind him was a ram caught in a thicket by its horns," so the sacrifice that God intended for Abraham to use was already there. God was the One, all along, Who provided the sacrifice that He intended for Abraham to make. The way had already been made. Abraham just discovered it after he passed the test.

Had Abraham failed the test, he would never have seen that God had already provided the lamb for the offering. Had Abraham failed to trust God, he would have missed the miracle. Had Abraham failed to believe God, he would have missed the blessing. Had Abraham failed to obey God, he would have missed the provision. Saints, God always has our ram in the bush, but we can miss it if we don't trust Him. God always has our ram in the bush, but if we don't believe Him, we can forfeit the blessing. God always has our ram in the bush, but if we don't obey Him, we can fumble the provision.

That's why if we are believers, we need to believe. That's why if we are saved, we have got to trust Him. And saints, that's why if we are going to walk with Him, we have got to obey Him.

He is YHWH-Yireh. He is the Lord our Provider. He is YHWH-Yireh, He is the Lord Who reveals. He is YHWH-Yireh, He is the Lord Who causes us to see. And he can never fail. He has to deliver 100 percent of the time. Why? Because God put the power in the Word to make itself come to pass. So as long as we sow our seed in good ground, protect it and water it, and keep the weeds out, it shall reproduce after its

#GodWillTestYouToBlessYou

kind. Why? Because it is a kingdom principle, and God put the power in the Word to make itself come to pass.

So Who is YHWH? YHWH is too much to process in your mind.

Who is YHWH? YHWH is too exhaustive to try to compartmentalize Him.

The best way to put it is that YHWH is the "I Am That I Am." YHWH is whoever you need Him to be. He is YHWH-Yireh, He is the Lord our Provider. He is YHWH-Yireh, He is the God Who *reveals*. He is YHWH-Yireh, He is the God Who *causes us to see it*.

So when the devil tries to tell you that God must want you to live from paycheck to paycheck, you can say, "Not so, you lying devil, for the Bible says that God opens up the windows of heaven for me and pours blessings on me that I don't have room enough to receive."

And when the devil tries to suggest that if God wanted you to prosper, He would have done it by now, you can say, "You are a liar, devil, for the Bible says that that, though He was rich, yet for my sake, He became poor, that I through His poverty might be rich."

And when the devil tries to tell you God wants you poor and quotes the Scripture, "for the poor you have with you always," you can say, "Get behind me, devil. First, He did not say that *I* had to be the poor, and second, the Bible says that He has made me be the head and not the tail, above and not beneath, a lender and not a borrower."

Jesus said, "After this manner pray, say, 'Hallowed be Your Name.'" If we want the manifestation of what the Name entails, we've got to hallow the Name. If we want the manifestation of what the Name promises, we have to hallow the Name. When we hallow the Name, we sow the Name. And the way we sow the Name is to speak the Name.

So we thank You, oh God, that You are *YHWH-Yireh*, the Lord our *Provider*. And we thank You, Lord, that You are YHWH-Yireh. You are the God Who *reveals* and causes us to see. Lord we give You praise, that You meet all our need according to Your riches in glory by Christ Jesus. And we bless You, O God, for causing us to see that You always have a ram in the bush. Thank You, Lord, that there is no good thing that You would withhold from us because we walk upright before You. And we magnify You, Lord, that because we bring all of our tithes to You in Your storehouse, that You open for us the windows of heaven, and pour such blessing upon us that we don't even have the room to store it all up.

You are YHWH-Yireh. You are our Provider. You are YHWH-Yireh. You cause us to see. And we do give You praise. In Jesus's Name.

#GodWillTestYouToBlessYou

CHAPTER 16

YHWH-NISSI—THE LORD OUR BANNER

#TheBattleIsNotYoursIt'sTheLord's

We are on the last leg of our journey in this comprehensive study of the Names of God.

The two Scripture references that we have relied on come respectively, from Exodus, chapter twenty, verse seven, and Luke chapter eleven, verse two.

Verse seven of the twentieth chapter of Exodus reads: "You shall not take the Name of the LORD your God in vain, for the LORD will not hold him guiltless who takes His Name in vain" (Exodus 20:7).

And in Luke, chapter eleven, verse two, Jesus gives us a model for prayer in response to a query from his disciples: "He said to them, "When you pray, say: Our Father in heaven, Hallowed be Your Name"" (Luke11:2).

In this study, God has revealed to us that there is a correlation between His commandment for us not to take the Name of the Lord in vain and Jesus's teaching that we are to deliberately and intentionally "hallow the Name" of the Lord.

We are expected to carry God's Name with purpose, and we do so when we embrace and tap into the power that is in the Name. To hallow God's Name is to sow His Name in the same way one would sow seed. And the way we sow the Name is by speaking the Name.

Now, on account of the kingdom principle of sowing and reaping, we understand that when we speak the Name of the Lord, we open the door for God to manifest the promise, because God put the power in the Word to make itself come to pass. This is a kingdom principle. Jesus Christ said, "So is the kingdom of God; it is as if a man should scatter seed on the ground."

God has given us access to His Name because God wants a personal relationship with us. We should, therefore, not settle for a "religious" experience with Him where we would only communicate with God when we need Him to do something. "Lord, would You heal my body." And when He heals me, that's it. I'm gone. That's where we only come to Him when we are in trouble. "Lord, would you get me out of this mess." And when He rescues me, that's it. I'm gone. That's where serving Him is somewhat of a "chore" or a "got to." "Got to" go to church. "Got to" pray. "Got to" pay tithes. "Got to" obey His Word. That's religion.

Jesus did not die so that we could be limited to a religious experience. They had religion before Christ came. Christ came so that we can have a personal relationship. When we talk about relationship, it is no longer "got to," it is "get to." We "get to" be God's favorite. We "get to" be the ones who He protects and preserves. We "get to" partake of His blessings and His miracles and His covenant. We "get to" access Him and spend time with Him and know Him.

DR. MELVIN G. BARNEY, ESQ.

And when you know YHWH, the devil can't make you feel like God is not going to come through for you. Because you know YHWH.

And when you know YHWH, the devil can't make you believe that God is not going to deliver you. Because you know YHWH.

And when you know YHWH, the devil can't make you think that God may have abandoned you. Because you know Him.

Saints, we've got to know Him, for the Scripture says that "the people who know their God shall be strong and carry out great exploits" (see Daniel 11:32). Let's get to know Him. He is YHWH.

And we have learned that YHWH is a mind-blowing God. YHWH is much too vast and much too complicated for words. When Moses was chosen to lead the people out of bondage, he asked God, "Who am I going to tell them You are?" And God said in response, "I Am That I Am. You don't have to fix it up. Just tell them I Am has sent you. The answer to your question is, 'I Just Am.'"

You might be looking for God to move one way, but instead, He moves another. You might be expecting God to do it the way He did it last time, but instead, He goes a whole different route and does it a whole different way.

You expect Him to catch it before it gets too late, but instead, He waits until it dies so He can raise it from the dead.

You expect Him to go with you into the battle, but instead, He tells you to stand on the sideline and praise Him while He confounds your enemies.

You expect Him to send you a whole lot of help to get the job done, but instead, He whittles your help down to a few, so it will be clear that the Lord did it.

#TheBattleIsNotYoursIt'sTheLord's

That's why you cannot try to box Him in. That's why you cannot try to get Him to do it your way. That's why you cannot counsel or instruct Him. You've got to let Him be Lord. He is YHWH!

And there are many dimensions to the Name YHWH. There are many angles to the Name YHWH. YHWH is multi-faceted, like a diamond. When you hold a diamond in the light and begin to turn it about, it will show you different things. Likewise, we are finding that the more we explore Him, the more YHWH reveals about Himself.

At this point, I want us to take a look at another revelation of YHWH, which is found in Exodus, chapter seventeen, verses fourteen through sixteen.

> Then the Lord said to Moses, "Write this for a memorial in the book and recount it in the hearing of Joshua, that I will utterly blot out the remembrance of Amalek from under heaven." And Moses built an altar and called its name, The-Lord-Is-My-Banner [*YHWH-Nissi*]; for he said, "Because the Lord has sworn: the Lord will have war with Amalek from generation to generation."
> Exodus 17:14-16, modified

The Bible says, "Thanks be to God [W]ho gives us the victory through our Lord Jesus Christ" (1 Corinthians 15:57). The Bible also says, "We are more than conquerors through Him [W]ho loved us" (Romans 8:37). No matter what the devil tries to do to you, you will always come out on top. Your victory, your preservation, your success is guaranteed.

Somebody may ask, "How did we get here? Why does persecution exist?" Unfortunately, when Adam sinned, he sold us all out (the entire human race) to the enemy; and on account of Adam's sin, we were all born into the kingdom of the devil.

It is because the devil reigns over the worldly system that there exists persecution, trouble, evil, burdens, and problems. The negative and destructive influences that exist are not of God and are not of God's kingdom. The Bible says, "The kingdom of God [consists of] righteousness and peace and joy in the Holy Spirit" (Romans 14:17). Thus, everything that is destructive, everything that is negative, every source of pain and sorrow, and everything that is contrary to righteousness, peace, and joy in the Holy Spirit come from Satan and the worldly kingdom over which he rules.

Citizenship in the devil's kingdom was not a choice we made. This was the default position caused by Adam. And because this is the default position, it does not require a choice to live for the devil. That's automatic. We were born in sin and shaped in iniquity (see Psalm 51:5).

But we can opt out of the devil's kingdom. We can choose to get out of Satan's kingdom, and we can choose, instead, to be subjects of God's kingdom. We can choose not to follow the devil and not to allow him to reign over us or control our lives. That requires a knowing, volitional decision.

And the way we opt *out* of Satan's kingdom is by volitionally opting *into* God's kingdom. When we choose to accept Christ as our Lord and Savior and make the volitional decision to live for God and follow Him, we have opted out of the devil's kingdom; and the result is that God will "deliver us from the power of darkness [which is the devil's kingdom], and convey [or transfer] us into the kingdom of

#TheBattleIsNotYoursIt'sTheLord's

the Son of His love [which is God's kingdom]" (Colossians 1:13, modified).

But let me say this: whenever it was that you actually made the decision to reject the devil and live for Christ, the enemy did not like it. When you made the decision to leave him and make Jesus your Lord instead, the devil was not happy. And particularly since he refuses to accept the fact that you meant business when you left him, Satan does everything he can to get you to walk away from God. He comes after you in order to get back at God.

And one of the strategies the enemy uses to get you to back away from God is to apply pressure or persecute you.

But even though Satan may launch an attack against you from time to time, he cannot get past God to get to you. And even though the devil may come after you with the intent to destroy you, God will always bring you out in victory. And even though Satan tries to take you out with the best he's got, God will always cause you to triumph.

In this chapter, we are talking about *YHWH-Nissi*, the Lord our *Banner*.

At this point, I want to look at the derivation of the Hebrew word *Nissi*, and how it has come to be translated "banner," and the symbolism behind that translation.

Nissi As Refuge

The translators of the *Septuagint* (which is the ancient Greek translation of the Old Testament scriptures) believed *nis·si'* to be derived from *nus*, which means "flee for refuge." And from this belief, they rendered YHWH-Nissi as "the Lord my Refuge."

A refuge is defined as a condition of being safe or sheltered from pursuit, danger, or trouble. A refuge is thus, shelter; a refuge is protection; a refuge is safety; a refuge is security.

Let's look at the ninety-first division of the Psalms, which gives us a picture of YHWH-Nissi as a refuge.

> He [W]ho dwells in the secret place of the Most High Shall abide under the shadow of the Almighty. I will say of the Lord, "He is my refuge and my fortress; My God, in Him I will trust." [...] You shall not be afraid of the terror by night, Nor of the arrow that flies by day, Nor of the pestilence that walks in darkness, Nor of the destruction that lays waste at noonday [...] For He shall give His angels charge over you, To keep you in all your ways. In their hands they shall bear you up, lest you dash your foot against a stone.
>
> Psalm 91:1-2, 5-6, 11-12

Nissi As Exultation

Getting back to our timeline on the derivation of *Nissi*, the translators of the *Vulgate* (which is a late fourth-century Latin translation of the Bible) supposed that *Nissi* was derived from *na·sas'*, which means "to hoist" or "lift up." And as a result of this thinking, *YHWH-Nissi* was rendered as "the Lord is my exaltation."

Exaltation is defined as the action of elevating someone in rank, power, or character. To exalt is to elevate by praise or in estimation. To exalt is to glorify, or to raise high, or to elevate.

#TheBattleIsNotYoursIt'sTheLord's

And in Isaiah, chapter fifty-nine, at the latter portion of verse nineteen, the Bible says, "When the enemy comes in like a flood, The Spirit of the Lord will lift up a standard against him" (see Isaiah 59:19).

Nissi As Standard or Banner

Notice here the Bible says, "Lift up a standard." Well, what is a standard? A standard is a banner or flag. And this brings us to the point where we were trying to get and to the question we need to ask.

What is the significance of a banner or flag, and why would God use that symbolism to describe Himself?

A banner is defined as a long strip of cloth bearing a slogan or design, hung in a public place or carried in a demonstration or procession. We have banners hanging around the church that bear the Names of God. Those banners bear a message. They are symbolic of something.

The flag of the United States of America is referred to as a "star-spangled banner" because a flag is a form of a banner. The US flag bears a message. It is symbolic of something.

When I was in my high school marching band (which, not to brag or anything, but which, at the time was the best band in the state of Ohio), whether we were marching in a parade or putting on a half-time show at a football game, or performing in an assembly, our processions were led by two young ladies who were bearing between them the banner of the Shaw High School Cardinal Marching Band. That banner carried a message.

Now let's talk about the symbolism and significance of a banner.

First, it identifies who you are or who you represent (i.e., High School Marching Band in a parade).

Second, it marks a territory that you claim a right to or that you may have discovered or settled (i.e., the California State Flag throughout the state).

Third, a standard raised in battle serves as a rallying point for armies (i.e., the US Flag in time of war).

Therefore, in essence, a banner or flag puts others on notice. When they see that banner, they are put on notice that this is the Mighty Cardinal Marching Band, or that this is California soil, or that this is the US Military. It also puts them on notice that all of the resources of the empire it represents are behind this flag, so, for example, when foreign enemies see the flag of the United States of America headed in their direction, they know that all the resources of the United States of America are behind that battalion.

So, when you say YHWH-Nissi, the Lord my Banner, this identifies who you are (I am a child of Covenant), whose you are (I belong to YHWH), and who you represent (I represent YHWH).

When you say YHWH-Nissi, the Lord my Banner, this marks a territory that you claim a right to or that you may have discovered or settled. For example, "I lay claim to everything that God has promised me, namely victory over the enemy."

When you say YHWH-Nissi, the Lord my Banner, this is a standard raised in battle, which serves as a rallying point for the armies of the Lord that are engaged in battle on your behalf. "We celebrate God for giving us the victory and causing us to triumph through Christ Jesus."

And when you declare that He is YHWH-Nissi, the Lord our Banner...

- This puts the enemy on notice that you are a child of the Most High God.

#TheBattleIsNotYoursIt'sTheLord's

- This puts the enemy on notice that you are in God, that God is in you, and that the battle is not yours, but it is the Lord's.
- And this puts the enemy on notice that all of the resources of heaven are behind you and that God is here to protect you, to preserve you, to sustain you, and to guarantee your victory!

Therefore, when you make the declaration that He is YHWH-Nissi and that He is your Banner, you are putting the enemy on notice that he has got to *get out*.

There are two things I want you to take from the fact that He is YHWH-Nissi, your Banner.

The first is this: you *do not* and *will not* have to fight a physical fight.

One of my favorite illustrations of this point is found in 2 Chronicles, when the Ammonites, the Moabites, and the inhabitants of Mount Seir came out to triple-team the people of God. Now, of course, the devil wanted them to be in fear and intimidated and nervous and question how they would be able to stand against three nations. But God wanted it to be clear to them that He is YHWH-Nissi, He would be their Banner, and God wanted them to know that He would fight this battle for them because the battle is not theirs, it's the Lord's.

In 2 Chronicles, chapter twenty, beginning from verse fourteen, the Bible says,

> Then the Spirit of the Lord came upon Jahaziel [...] And he said [...] Thus says the Lord to you: "Do not be afraid nor dismayed because of this great multitude, for the battle is not yours, but God's.

Tomorrow go down against them [...]
You will not need to fight in this battle."
2 Chronicles 20:14-17

Some of you spend all of your time fighting with folks, disagreeing with folks, bickering with folks, and arguing with folks. You need to cut that out. You need to stop it. You are lending yourself over to the devil. You are allowing yourself to be an instrument of the devil. Stop it. By giving the enemy license to use you, you are giving the enemy license to attack you, and you are tying God's hands so that He cannot protect you. And that's why you always find yourself in a mess, and that's why God can never rescue you.

You are overrun with conflict. Conflict at home. Conflict with your spouse. Conflict with your children. Conflict at your job. Conflict at your church. You need to stop it. The battle is not yours. Child of God, you do not have to fight a physical fight.

Getting back to our text, just as Jahaziel prophesied, God's people did not have to fight in that battle. The Bible says that on the next day, they went out, and instead of having them arm themselves with guns and cannons and grenades, King Jehoshaphat came up with a new war strategy.

Picking up in verse twenty-one of 2 Chronicles, chapter twenty, the Bible says:

> And when [Jehoshaphat] had consulted with the people, he appointed those who should sing to the Lord, and who should praise the beauty of holiness, as they went out before the army and were saying: "Praise the Lord, For His mercy endures forever." [And] when they began to sing

#TheBattleIsNotYoursIt'sTheLord's

and to praise, *the Lord set ambushes against the people* of Ammon, Moab, and Mount Seir, who had come against Judah; and they were defeated."

2 Chronicles 20:20-21,
emphasis added

As the people praised Him, the Lord set an ambush. The battle is not yours or mine. It is the Lord's.

To top things off as He does, the Bible says that after God fought for Israel and defeated their enemies, God left them with an extraordinarily bountiful blessing. Look at what the Bible says in verses twenty-four and twenty-five:

So when Judah came to a place overlooking the wilderness, they looked toward the multitude; and there *were* their dead bodies, fallen on the earth. No one had escaped. When Jehoshaphat and his people came to take away their spoil, they found among them an abundance of valuables on the dead bodies, and precious jewelry, which they stripped off for themselves, more than they could carry away; and they were three days gathering the spoil because there was so much.

2 Chronicles 20:24-25,
emphasis added

Your fight is not a physical fight. The physical fight is God's fight, and God does not fight fair.

The second thing you can take from the fact that He is YHWH-Nissi, your Banner, is this: you *do* have to fight a spiritual fight. Your fight is *not* a physical fight. But your fight is a *spiritual* fight.

The Bible says in the sixth chapter of Ephesians, in verses ten to twelve:

> Finally, my brethren, be strong in the Lord and in the power of His might. Put on the whole armor of God, that you may be able to stand against the wiles of the devil. For we do not wrestle against flesh and blood, but against principalities, against powers, against the rulers of the darkness of this age, against spiritual hosts of wickedness in the heavenly places.
>
> Ephesians 6:10-12

Because He is YHWH-Nissi, God has made it His business to fight our battles for us. Therefore, saints, our part in this battle is *not* physical. But that does not mean we should run and hide, because faith without works is dead. And that does not mean that we are to sit at the bus stop and do nothing, because faith without works is dead. At the very least, we may have to get dressed for the battle.

Nevertheless, God wants us to see that our part in this battle is *not* physical. Our part in this battle is *not* against the people who get on our nerves. Our part in this battle is *not* against the people who set up snares and traps in our pathway. That's God's part. God will take care of them. Our part in this battle is spiritual.

Exodus, chapter seventeen, captures an incident when Amalek had come out to pick a fight against the people of God. Now keep in mind, the Amalekites were distant cousins

#TheBattleIsNotYoursItsTheLord's

of Israel's. Whereas the Israelites were descendants of Jacob, Amalek was a descendant of Jacob's twin brother Esau, and the Amalekites had an issue with Israel on account of the theft by Jacob of Esau's birthright and blessing. So even though Esau had forgiven Jacob and let that go hundreds of years ago, his descendants had not. Thus, there was constant tension between the two nations. And so here, the Amalekites came out to fight against Israel when they were in the wilderness trying to make their way to the promised land.

Now, the Bible says that at first, Moses had charged Joshua, who at that time was the captain of the troops, to go out and engage in a physical battle with Amalek. But it soon became evident that there was a problem with this war strategy (see Exodus 17:9-16). This war strategy would contemplate that Israel could defeat the enemy in the flesh, and this war strategy would contemplate that they could defeat the enemy in their own strength; but remember, God is trying to teach us that the battle is not ours, it's the Lord's. God wants us to see that it is God Who always gives us victory. God wants us to see that it is God Who always causes us to triumph.

So Moses instructed Joshua to choose men from the army and go down to fight against Amalek, but then Moses also said, "I will stand on the top of the hill with the rod of God in my hand" (Exodus 17:9). Now, let me briefly deal with the symbolism of the rod of God. The rod of God was a symbol of the Word of God. Moses was saying, in essence, my weapon for this battle will be the Word of God.

And likewise, people of God, you have got to recognize that the weapons God has given you are not carnal. Yours is not a physical fight because the battle is not yours. The battle is the Lord's. The Bible says while Joshua was down there engaged in all that fighting, it did not mean "a hill of beans."

When we look at the Scripture, the Bible says in verse eleven, "And so it was, when Moses held up his hand, that Israel prevailed; and when he let down his hand, Amalek prevailed." Do you see that? It was the Word that was getting them the victory. Why? Because God put the power in the Word to make itself come to pass. It is a kingdom principle.

Likewise, with you, it will be the Word, it will be your faith, it will be your praise that will guarantee you victory. Why? Because God put the power in the Word to make itself come to pass. It is a kingdom principle.

And beginning at verse twelve of Exodus, chapter seventeen, the Bible says, "But Moses' hands *became* heavy..." (Exodus 17:12).

Sometimes you may get tired. Sometimes you may get weary. But that's why it is always good to have the saints in your corner, holding you up.

The Bible goes on to say,

> [S]o they took a stone and put it under [Moses], and he sat on it. And Aaron and Hur supported his hands, one on one side, and the other on the other side; and his hands were steady until the going down of the sun. So that's how Joshua defeated Amalek and his people with the edge of the sword. Then the Lord said to Moses, "Write this for a memorial..."
> Exodus 17:9-16, modified

God's message to the believer is, "I am YHWH-Nissi. I will always fight your battles for you. I will always handle your enemies for you. I will always defend and protect you. The battle is not yours. It is the Lord's."

#TheBattleIsNotYoursItsTheLord's

That's why if we are believers, we need to believe. That's why if we claim to trust God, we need to trust Him. God will never leave you alone to fight your own battles. God will never abandon you or allow you to go under. The more the enemy tries to persecute you, the more God stands up for you and gives you victory. You don't have to fight a physical fight. You are charged to stand still and see the salvation of the Lord. You are charged to hold your peace and let YHWH fight your battles. You are charged to stay out of the physical battles and engage in the spiritual battles. Your weapons are the Word, prayer, and praise. If you do that, God will always give you victory. If you do that, God will always cause you to triumph. If you do that, God will always make sure you win.

He is YHWH-Nissi, He is the Lord our Banner. He is YHWH-Nissi, He is the Lord our Refuge. He is YHWH-Nissi, He is the Lord our Protector. And because He fights your battles for you, you cannot lose. You always win. You always triumph. You always get the victory. You always come out on top. Why? Because He is YHWH-Nissi, and God put the power in the Word to make itself come to pass.

Who is YHWH? YHWH is too complex to figure out. Who is YHWH? YHWH is too complicated to try to understand. The best way to put it is that YHWH is the "I Am That I Am." YHWH is whoever you need Him to be. He is YHWH-Nissi, He is the Lord our Banner.

So when the devil tries to tell you that the enemy is going to take you out, you can say, "Not so, devil, for He is YHWH-Nissi, He is the Lord Who fights my battles."

And when the devil tries to tell you that there is no way you are getting out of this mess, you can say, "You are a liar devil, for He is YHWH-Nissi, He is the Lord Who gives me the victory."

DR. MELVIN G. BARNEY, ESQ.

And when the devil tries to tell you that God has left you hanging and that He is not coming back for you, you can say, "Get behind me, devil, for He is YHWH-Nissi, He is the Lord my refuge, and He always causes me to triumph."

Jesus said, "After this manner pray, say, 'Hallowed be Your Name.'" If we want the manifestation of what the Name entails, we've got to hallow the Name. If we want the manifestation of what the Name promises, we have to hallow the Name. When we hallow the Name, we sow the Name. And the way we sow the Name is to speak the Name.

So we thank You, oh God, that You are YHWH-Nissi. You are the Lord our Banner. And we thank You, Lord, that You are YHWH-Nissi. You are the Lord our Refuge.

Thank You, God, that because we dwell in the secret place of the Most High, that we get to abide under the shadow of the Almighty. Thank You for being our refuge and our fortress and for being the God in whom we can put our trust. Thank You for always delivering us from the snare of the fowler and from the perilous pestilence. Thank You that you cover us with Your feathers and that it is under Your wings that we can take refuge. Lord, we praise You that we don't have to be afraid of the terror by night, nor of the arrow that flies by day, nor of the pestilence that walks in darkness, nor of the destruction that lays waste at noonday. You cause a thousand to fall at our side and ten thousand at our right hand, but You don't allow any of those things to come near us. Thank You, Lord, that You won't allow any evil to befall us, and You are not going to let any plague come near our dwelling. We bless You, God, for giving Your angels charge over us and for requiring them to keep us in all our ways.

You are *YHWH-Nissi*, the Lord our *Banner*. You are YHWH-Nissi. You are the Lord our Refuge. You always give us victory in Christ Jesus. You always cause us to triumph in

#TheBattleIsNotYoursIt'sTheLord's

Christ Jesus. You make us more than conquerors in Christ Jesus. In You, we always win and can never lose because You are YHWH-Nissi, You are the Lord our Banner. In Jesus's Name.

CHAPTER 17

YHWH-ROHI—THE LORD OUR SHEPHERD

#OurRideOrDieGod

Well, here we are, about to land this plane, where we have engaged in an exhaustive study of the Names of God. The two Scripture references that we have drawn from come from Exodus, chapter twenty, verse seven, and from Luke, chapter eleven, verse two.

Let's go first to Exodus, chapter twenty, verse seven: "You shall not take the Name of the LORD your God in vain, for the LORD will not hold him guiltless who takes His Name in vain" (Exodus 20:7).

And now let's go to Luke, chapter eleven and verse two, where Jesus gives this model for prayer to those of us who have transferred into God's kingdom: "He said to them, 'When you pray, say: Our Father in heaven, Hallowed be Your Name'" (Luke 11:2).

God has revealed how His Name applies to the kingdom principle of sowing and reaping. We are being urged not to take the Name of the Lord for granted but instead to use the Name of the Lord as a resource and a tool to cause the blessings of God, and the promises of the Word, and the will of God to manifest in our lives.

God has given us access to His Name and authorized us to sow it, just as one given a natural seed would sow that seed. On account of the kingdom principle of sowing and reaping, when we sow the Name by speaking it, and hallowing it, and believing it and embracing it, and holding on to it, it reproduces after its kind, and we reap what the Name promises, because God put the power in the Name to make itself come to pass. Again, this is a kingdom principle. Jesus Christ said it this way: "So is the kingdom of God: it is as if a man should scatter seed on the ground."

By instructing us not to carry His Name in vain and teaching us to hallow His Name, God is demonstrating that we do not have to limit ourselves to a religious experience with Him. God wants us to pursue an intimate, personal relationship with Him. We need to know Him.

When you know YHWH, the devil can't make you doubt how much you mean to Him. Because you know YHWH.

And when you know YHWH, the devil can't make you believe that God has abandoned you. Because you know YHWH.

And when you know YHWH, the devil can't make you think that God is hostile toward you. Because you know Him.

The Scripture says that "the people who know their God shall be strong and carry out great exploits" (see Daniel 11:32). The people of God ought to know Him. He is YHWH.

And we have learned that YHWH is a complex God. YHWH is a God whose ways are past finding out.

DR. MELVIN G. BARNEY, ESQ.

You might be looking for God to act one way, but instead, He acts in a different way. You might be expecting God to go about it in this way, but instead, He goes about it in a whole different way.

You expect to be healed as a result of somebody laying hands on you or praying over you or anointing you with oil, but instead, the Lord instructs them to tell you to go and dip seven times in the nastiest, most polluted body of water in the land in order to get your healing.

You expect God to keep your baby away from the pharaoh who sought to kill him, but instead, He causes the Pharaoh's daughter to rescue your child and adopt him and pay you to raise him for her.

You wondered if God had abandoned you since you were imprisoned for something that you didn't even do, but instead, He uses that jail experience to set you up to be the prime minister over the nation of Egypt.

That's why you cannot try to box God in, or get Him to do it your way, counsel Him, or instruct Him. You've got to let God be God. He is YHWH!

And as we have learned, there are many dimensions of YHWH. YHWH is multi-faceted, like a diamond. We are finding that the more we explore Him, the more YHWH reveals about Himself.

For this encounter that we are going to study, let's go to the twenty-third number of the Psalms and look at verse one where we are introduced to *YHWH-Rohi*, the Lord our *Shepherd*: "The Lord is my Shepherd [*YHWH-Rohi*]; I shall not want" (Psalm 23:1).

The Scriptures are flooded with metaphors, similes, allegories, parables, and word pictures that God uses in order to provide His people with something they can relate to. His

#OurRideOrDieGod

intent is to teach us life lessons, and He uses these mechanisms to get His point across to us.

For example, God says, "You are the light of the world," to teach us purpose.

And God says, "You are the salt of the earth," to point out our significance.

One of my favorites that He says is "The sower sows the word," which He uses to teach us the kingdom principle of sowing and reaping.

It is very common for God to use metaphors, similes, allegories, parables, and word pictures to speak to us.

And a very popular metaphor, simile, word picture that the Lord uses to describe his people is to compare us with "sheep."

In the one-hundredth division of the Psalms, at verse three, the Bible says, "Know that the Lord, He is God; It is He Who has made us, and not we ourselves; We are His people and the sheep of His pasture" (Psalm 100:3).

Also, in John, chapter twenty-one, Jesus tells Peter very emphatically to feed, tend to, and take care of His sheep.

> Jesus said to Simon Peter, "Simon, *son* of Jonah, do you love Me more than these?" He said to Him, "Yes, Lord; You know that I love You." He said to him, "Feed My lambs." He said to him again a second time, "Simon, *son* of Jonah, do you love Me?" He said to Him, "Yes, Lord; You know that I love You." He said to him, "Tend My sheep." He said to him the third time, "Simon, *son* of Jonah, do you love Me?" Peter was grieved because He said to him the third time, "Do you

love Me?" And he said to Him, "Lord, You know all things; You know that I love You." Jesus said to him, "Feed My sheep.
John 21:15-17

From these references, I want to address two things that stick out prominently. The first is that God clearly refers to His people as sheep. The scripture we read says, "We are His people, the sheep of His pasture" (Psalm 100:3). The second is that God is serious about the care of His sheep. In that particular discourse from John, chapter twenty-one, that Jesus had with Peter, He said to him three times, "Peter, if you love Me, I need you to do this for Me: this is important to me. I need to be able to count on you: feed My sheep, tend My sheep, take care of My sheep." He is a "Ride-or-Die" kind of God.

Here, and throughout the Scriptures, God describes and identifies and refers to His people as sheep.

Let's talk about a few observations that we can make about sheep, which may shed some light on why our "Ride-or-Die" God was so insistent that Peter look after them, and why God makes sure His sheep have a caretaker.

Observations about Sheep

1.   Sheep Require A Great Deal of Attention

A first observation I would like to make about sheep is that they require a great deal of attention, particularly as compared to other livestock. Sheep do not have a good sense of direction; they have been known to wander. It is not uncommon for sheep to get lost. Another interesting thing about sheep is that sometimes they can have a hard time

#OurRideOrDieGod

203

locating food and water on their own. Sheep require a great deal of attention to survive the snares and traps of the enemy, and this may account for one reason that God makes sure His sheep have a caretaker.

2. Sheep are Defenseless and Vulnerable

A second observation about sheep is that they are defenseless and vulnerable. Sheep do not appear to be able to fight off their predators. You never see sheep snarling or hissing when they sense danger. I ran across an article called "About Sheep," found at www.ciwf.com, which states that "sheep are prey animals and are largely defenseless against predators, naturally nervous, and easily frightened. [It goes on to say] They flock together for safety."

The fact that sheep are defenseless and vulnerable to the attack of the enemy would be another reason that God wants to make sure that His sheep have a caretaker.

3. Sheep Are Leery of Strangers, but They Will Follow Their Leader without Hesitation

Something else I have learned about sheep, which is even highlighted in the Scripture, is that sheep are very leery of strangers, but they will follow their leader without hesitation.

According to sheep101.info, "Sheep have a strong instinct to follow the sheep in front of them. When one sheep decides to go somewhere, the rest of the flock usually follows, even if it is not a good 'decision.' For example, sheep will follow each other to slaughter. If one sheep jumps over a cliff, the others are likely to follow."

The fact that sheep will keep their distance from a stranger, but will follow their leader, be it the sheep that is in front of them, or be it their shepherd, would be another reason that God is so intent on making sure that His sheep have a caretaker.

These observations that we can note about sheep would account for why Jesus addresses their need for a loving, protective, "Ride-or-Die" shepherd. In the Gospel according to John, in chapter ten, the Bible says, beginning from verse one:

> Most assuredly, I say to you, he who does not enter the sheepfold by the door, but climbs up some other way, the same is a thief and a robber. But he who enters by the door is the shepherd of the sheep. To him the doorkeeper opens, and the sheep hear his voice; and he calls his own sheep by name and leads them out. And when he brings out his own sheep, he goes before them; and the sheep follow him, for they know his voice. Yet they will by no means follow a stranger, but will flee from him, for they do not know the voice of strangers.
>
> John 10:1-5

Jesus notes in His explanation about the proclivities of sheep that there exists a relationship between a shepherd and his sheep, in which the sheep will respond to their shepherd. Although sheep are known as timid creatures, and although they are hesitant and distrustful, and although they are suspecting and fearful, sheep will, in spite of and contrary to their

#OurRideOrDieGod

norm of behavior, hear the voice of their shepherd, know the voice of their shepherd, and follow their own "Ride-or-Die" shepherd as he goes before them.

Now let's make some observations about a good shepherd, and take a look at what it is about the "Ride-or-Die" God that draws in the sheep. For that purpose, we need to go back to the twenty-third number of the Psalms and read verses one through six, which establish the parameters and set the example of good shepherding by YHWH-Rohi, the Chief Shepherd.

> The Lord is my Shepherd; I shall not want. He makes me to lie down in green pastures; He leads me beside the still waters. He restores my soul; He leads me in the paths of righteousness for His Name's sake. Yea, though I walk through the valley of the shadow of death, I will fear no evil; for You are with me; Your rod and Your staff, they comfort me. You prepare a table before me in the presence of my enemies; You anoint my head with oil; My cup runs over. Surely goodness and mercy shall follow me all the days of my life; and I will dwell in the house of the Lord forever.
>
> Psalm 23:1-6

In verse one of the twenty-third Psalm, the Bible gives us to know that because He is YHWH-Rohi, you shall not want. Now that is not prohibiting us from desiring things, which may be how we would define it in today's vernacular. In that context, the word "want" means God will never allow you to be in a state of want. In other words, it means He will not allow you to lack, or be empty, or do without, or be deprived of, or have a deficiency. Because the Lord is your Shepherd, you don't have to lack, you don't have to do without, you don't have to be deprived; He will not allow you to have a deficiency. You shall not want.

In verse two, the Bible says, "He makes me to lie down [and dwell] in green pastures; He leads me beside the still waters."

The second point is this. Because He is YHWH-Rohi, your Shepherd, it is He Who will always bring you to a place of rest and comfort. He will always bring you to a place of abundance and sufficiency. He will always lead you to a place of nourishment, and He will always lead you to a place of refreshing. He is YHWH-Rohi. He makes you lie down in green pastures, and He leads you besides the still waters.

Verse three says this: "He restores your soul; and will lead you in the paths of righteousness for His Name's sake."

Point number three: because He is YHWH-Rohi, your Shepherd, you can rest assured that He will restore your soul. Remember, your soul consists of your mind, your will, your emotions, and your intellect, and it is your soul that serves as the battleground of the devil.

The devil works overtime on you to get you to doubt God. The devil tries to get you in unbelief and undermine your faith. He tries to talk you into walking by sight and not by faith. But the Bible says that YHWH-Rohi, your Shepherd, steps in and restores your soul that has been under attack. That means He will renew your mind. That means He teaches you how to think, and He teaches you "right thinking." That means He shows you how to yield to Him and how to subject your will to His will. That means He works on your thoughts so that you will be anxious for nothing.

#OurRideOrDieGod

207

That means He does not lead you astray, but He leads you down the right paths and instructs you in ways of righteousness and safety. He is YHWH-Rohi, the Lord our Shepherd.

Then it goes on in verse four to say, "Yea, though I walk through the valley of the shadow of death, I will fear no evil; For You are with me; Your rod and Your staff, they comfort me."

The fourth point is this: no matter what you go through, you can know that YHWH-Rohi is with you. And because you know He is with you, you know you will always be protected. You know you will always be preserved. You know you will always be safeguarded because there is nothing too hard for the Lord. The Bible says, "If God be for us, who can be against us?" (Romans 8:31). Because YHWH-Rohi is with you, you do not have to fear anything.

Then it goes on to say that the rod and the staff of God comfort you. Now, remember, a shepherd's rod is an offensive weapon that he uses to fight off any predators that would come after the sheep. And his staff is a post that has a hook on the end, which the shepherd uses to guide the sheep that may be wandering or straying. As we have learned, in the Bible, the rod is a symbol of the Word of God, and the staff represents the ministry of the Holy Spirit to lead and guide us.

So, because He is YHWH-Rohi, you know He's got your back. He's not going to let anything happen to you, and He will always guide you to safety because He is YHWH-Rohi, your Shepherd. "When the enemy comes in like a flood, The Spirit of the Lord will lift up a standard against him" (Isaiah 59:19). "The Lord will guide you continually, And satisfy your soul in drought, And strengthen your bones; You shall be like a watered garden, And like a spring of water, whose waters do not fail" (Isaiah 58:11).

He's not going to let the enemy take you out because He is YHWH-Rohi, your Shepherd.

Verse five says, "You prepare a table before me in the presence of my enemies; You anoint my head with oil; My cup runs over."

The next point is that after He has done all of that, He will turn around and force your enemies to look on as witnesses while He causes you to feast and abound in His sufficiency. They may not like you, but they see what great things the Lord is doing for you. They might talk about you, but they see the blessing of God all over everything you do. They may envy you, but they see you walking in the grace of God.

He prepares a table before you, all up in the presence of your enemies.

And then He goes on to anoint your head with oil. The anointing of oil in this context represents the fat of the land. This stands for abundance, blessing, bounty, divine favor, and prosperity.

He pours it all over you and heaps it upon you until you cannot even contain it. The Scripture says, "My cup runs over." That's overflow. That's abundance. That's the blessing. That's more than enough. That is El Shaddai, the God *Who is More Than Enough*.

Finally, in verse six, the Bible says, "Surely goodness and mercy shall follow me all the days of my life; And I will dwell in the house of the LORD forever" (Psalm 23:6).

Because He is YHWH-Rohi, your Shepherd, you get to bask in God's *chesed*. *Chesed* is the Hebrew word that describes God's lovingkindness. David said, "Because Your lovingkindness [*chesed*] is better than life, my lips shall praise You. Thus I will bless You while I live; I will lift up my hands in Your Name" (Psalm 63:3-4, modified).

#OurRideOrDieGod

God's *chesed* accounts for the bounty of benefits to you. God's *chesed* is responsible for all of that grace to you. God's *chesed* explains the reason for all of these blessings on you. God's *chesed* gives rise to all of this favor on you.

Somebody ought to give God the praise for His mercy and His grace because "It is of the Lord's mercies that we are not consumed, because His compassions fail not" (Lamentations 3:22, KJV).

He is YHWH-Rohi. He is the Lord our Shepherd. He is YHWH-Rohi, He is the Lord Who looks after you. He is YHWH-Rohi, He is the Lord Who takes care of you.

And because He looks out for you, when it looks like you should be losing, He steps in and causes you to win. And because He takes care of you, when it looks like you should be hungry, He causes you to eat of the good of the land. Why? Because He is YHWH-Rohi, and God put the power in the Word to make itself come to pass.

So Who is YHWH? YHWH is too intricate to wrap your mind around. Who is YHWH? YHWH is too deep to be able to keep up with. The best way to put it is that YHWH is the "I Am That I Am." YHWH is whoever you need Him to be. He is YHWH-Rohi, He is the Lord our Shepherd.

So when the devil tries to convince you that you are not going to make it, you can say, "Not today, devil, for He is YHWH-Rohi, and He won't allow me to be in want."

And when the devil tries to get you in fear that the predators are going to destroy you, you can say, "No, no, devil, for He is YHWH-Rohi, and I've got His rod, which is His Word, and His Staff, the Holy Spirit, to protect me."

And when the devil tries to make you feel like an outcast, or make you feel like a misfit, or make you feel like you missed your opportunity, you can say, "Get behind me, devil, for He is YHWH-Rohi, He is My Shepherd, and I am basking in His goodness, and I am basking in His grace."

Jesus said, "After this manner pray, say, 'Hallowed be Your Name.'"

If we want the manifestation of what the Name entails, we've got to hallow the Name. If we want the manifestation of what the Name promises, we have to hallow the Name. When we hallow the Name, we sow the Name. And the way we sow the Name is to speak the Name.

So we thank You, O God, that You are YHWH-Rohi. You are the Lord our Shepherd. And we thank You, Lord, that You are YHWH-Rohi. You are the Lord Who looks after us. Thank You, God, that You will never allow us to be in want, and You will never allow us to go without.

You are YHWH-Rohi. You are the God Who regulates our minds, and You are the One Who regulates our thoughts so that they always remain on You and so that we will always come out on top. Thank You for Your *chesed*, Your lovingkindness, for truly it is better than life.

And we thank You for your mercy and grace, which are the reasons that we are still standing today.

You are YHWH-Rohi. You are the Lord our Shepherd. You are YHWH-Rohi. You are the Lord our Caretaker. And we love You today with all of our hearts. In Jesus's Name. Hallelujah. Amen.

CHAPTER 18

DOES ORDER MATTER?

#Don'tNecessarilySaveTheBestForLast

Exodus, chapter twenty, verse seven, says: "You shall not take the Name of the LORD your God in vain, for the LORD will not hold him guiltless who takes His Name in vain" (Exodus 20:7).

And in the Gospel of Luke, chapter eleven and verse two, the Bible says: "He said to them, 'When you pray, say: Our Father in heaven, Hallowed be Your Name'" (Luke11:2).

This chapter concludes our teaching on the Names of God and examination of the fact that we, the people of God, have been given the Names of the Lord to use as a tool to manifest the will of God in our lives and as a resource to cause the promises of God to come to pass in our lives.

The kingdom principle of sowing and reaping applies even to the Names of the Lord, such that when we open up our mouths and speak the Name of the Lord, we usher in the power of God to manifest the promises that the Name stands for. Why? Because God put the power in the Name to make itself come to pass. This is a kingdom principle. Jesus Christ said it this way: "So is the kingdom of God, it is as if a man should scatter seed on the ground."

Thus, when we engage the Name of the Lord in our affairs, use it as a tool, sow it as a seed, and put into practice what this book teaches, we are not taking the Name of the Lord our God in vain but utilizing it the way God intends: as a tool to manifest the will of God in our lives and as a resource to cause the promises of God to come to pass in our lives.

Now, I understand that this is a lot to take in. And when we consider the Names of the Lord in all of their dimensions and facets, there are two closely related questions that I get on occasion. The first is whether any of the Names is more powerful or more important or more useful than the others? And the second is whether the order in which we invoke the Names really matters?

To address the first of these questions, let's consider 1 Corinthians, chapter twelve, verse thirty-one, where the Bible encourages us to "earnestly desire the best gifts."

Now let me just point out that I am aware of the context. The *context* under which Paul gave this *concept* of "coveting what is best" is in the *context* of the spiritual gifts. However, the reason I want to draw from this concept here is because I think the concept of going after or pursuing the best is actually universal. This concept is not limited to the context of spiritual gifts but certainly applies to our drawing upon or sowing the Names of the Lord as well.

When we examine the Names of the Lord in all of their dimensions and facets, the answer to the first question is dynamic. The Name that is more powerful or important or useful, or, in other words, which is the "best," will be the Name that speaks to the issue that is before us at any given time. To the person in a financial crisis, YHWH-Yireh is the "best." But to the person who just received a dire health prognosis, YHWH-Rapha would be the "best." So the Name that is the "best" will be constantly changing depending on the circumstances.

With respect to the second question of whether order really matters, I think it does.

To me, revealing the Names of the Lord in a certain order is like taking a journey into the presence of God, akin to entering into the temple or tabernacle of God, where, once you get there, you have access to the blessings of God.

A study of the tabernacle of God that Moses had been given the blueprints for reveals that it had layers. There was the courtyard on the outskirts, and there was a sanctuary within. The inner part, the sanctuary, was divided into a Holy Place and a Most Holy Place, where the presence of God dwelled. The layers within the tabernacle that a person had access to would depend on who you were, what your assignment was, and how close you were to God. And the constant that applied to everybody, no matter who you were, was that everybody had to start on the outside and work their way into the place where they could obtain the blessing.

My approach to teaching the Names of God is similar. You start on the outside and work your way through the levels.

When I teach the Names, I start with the titles, Elohiym and El Shaddai, and talk about the differences between a title and a name. I point out the fact that a title is generic and kind of distant, whereas a name is personal and intimate. God's titles, Elohiym and El Shaddai, are like standing in the outer courtyard of the tabernacle of God. That's the place everybody could access. That's where they would all bring their sacrifices, but there wasn't anything particularly exclusive about the courtyard. Like a title, this was the place

#Don'tNecessarilySaveTheBestForLast

that was distant. Like a title, there was no intimacy in the courtyard.

The people who were intimate with God and who had relationships with God and whose assignments required them to have special access were given access to places inside the tabernacle that were off-limits to others. These people could go beyond the courtyard of the tabernacle, into the sanctuary, and find themselves on the pathway to the presence of God.

This would relate to how I teach the Name YHWH. YHWH, the personal Name of God, would be like the gateway that allows you access into the sanctuary. Everybody did not have the right to access the sanctuary. The Holy Place was off-limits to all but a few, and the Most Holy Place was off-limits to all but one. Likewise, everybody does not have the right to access the Name YHWH as a resource. Remember what God told Moses? "I appeared unto your fathers Abraham, Isaac, and Jacob as El Shaddai, but by My Name YHWH, I was not known to them" (Exodus 6:3, modified).

It was in the Holy Place of the sanctuary where outlying ministry to the Lord occurred. Common folk could not go there—you had to have a right of access. People who were unclean or unrighteous or unwashed or contaminated could not enter the sanctuary; you had to have a right to be there. But before you could pass through the gate and enter into the Holy Place, you had to wash yourself in the bronze laver. Any unauthorized person who tried to enter the sanctuary, or any authorized person who tried to gain access without first having washed in the bronze laver, would die. That laver served as the cleansing basin to allow access.

Likewise, in a sense, YHWH-T'Sidkenu, our Righteousness, and YHWH-M'Kaddesh, our Sanctification, serve as the cleansing basins that qualify us for entry and facilitate our access to the next level by ratifying in us who we are in Christ.

In order to fully receive what God desires for us, we must first have a correct understanding of *who we are in Christ* and *what rights we have*, and of the fact that we are supposed to have a personal relationship with God, not just a religious experience with Him. You have to know that God has cleansed you, made you righteous, sanctified you, and favored you. That groundwork has to be made before we can believe God for the miracles and the promises.

Hallowing YHWH-T'Sidkenu causes us to reflect on the fact that God Himself cleaned us up and made us righteous in Him. This liberates us from the burden of condemnation that drives us to hide from God. As we hallow His Name as YHWH-M'Kaddesh, we are reminded that we are highly favored of God. We are important to God. He chose us, hand-picked us, and gave us unmerited rights and entitlements to His blessings just because He loves us.

YHWH-T'Sidkenu and YHWH-M'Kaddesh address *our position in God*, which helps to shore up our thinking as to who we are in Christ and what are our rights and entitlements to the blessings of God.

It is important for us to have those issues addressed and squared away and to know our position in Him before we try to pray for things like the miracle of healing.

If I try to jump to YHWH-Rapha, and I want to pray the Lord my Healer, without having first addressed my righteous stance in Him, or who I am in Christ, or what are my rights and entitlements, then when I get over into YHWH-Rapha, I'm going to have to contend with doubt. "Maybe the Lord will heal me," or "If it's His will to heal me," or "Maybe it's going to work," or "Maybe God does not want that for me," or, "Maybe it's not God's will for me…" And according

#Don'tNecessarilySaveTheBestForLast

to the Bible, that's the sort of doubting and wavering that prohibits us from receiving from God.

> [L]et him ask in faith, with no doubting, for he who doubts is like a wave of the sea driven and tossed by the wind. For let not that man suppose that he will receive anything from the Lord; *he is* a double-minded man, unstable in all his ways.
>
> James 1:6-8

We have to know who we are positionally in order to be able to lock into the faith that's necessary to receive the things God has promised us.

That's why I teach we should hallow YHWH-T'Sidkenu and YHWH-M'Kaddesh before the other facets of His Name. YHWH-T'Sidkenu and YHWH-M'Kaddesh address our position in God.

From there, we go to YHWH-Shalom and YHWH-Shammah, which address *God's position in us.*

YHWH-Shalom and YHWH-Shammah give us the revelation of the spirit of God, the power of God, at work on the inside of us because of our position in Him. Hallowing His Name, YHWH-Shalom, causes us to internalize the fact that He is the Lord our Peace. His is a perfect peace that rises up inside you when the enemy would want you to be shattered, nervous, upset, and running around in fear. And then when you hallow the Name, YHWH-Shammah, you recognize Him as God living inside you. "Christ in you the hope of glory" (Colossians 1:27). "For it is God who works in you both to will and to do for His good pleasure" (Philippians 2:13). "Greater is He that is in you, than he who is in the world" (see 1 John 4:4).

In our tabernacle illustration, all of this is going on in the Holy Place, inside the sanctuary. However, now that you have addressed who you are in Him and Who He is in you, you are ready to advance to the next level. You are ready to receive. Now you can believe God for the miracles and the promises. There is no issue with condemnation. You know who you are in Christ. You recognize that God is working in you. Your faith has been fortified, and you are ready for whatever God has for you.

In the tabernacle illustration, that would advance you to the final level, allowing you to pass through the veil, enter into the Holy of Holies, and go up to the ark of the covenant where all of these goodies have been stored up.

And at this point, when it comes to things like praying for healing, you are confident that your prayers are heard and that your requests are granted because you know what He has promised you and where you stand with Him.

And when it comes to praying for provision, you know God is moving on your behalf. You are confident that your harvest is on the way and that you will receive everything He promised. Your faith is intact, and you know God cannot lie.

YHWH-Rapha and YHWH-Yireh, deal with some of the goodies found in the Holy of Holies that benefit you. Things that affect your well-being. Things that affect your quality of life. Things that affect your survival. Your healing. Your provision. The goodies that benefit you.

So now that you are in a position to receive the promises, miracles, and blessings, we can cap it off with the last two facets of God's multi-faceted Name. Hallowing YHWH-Nissi and YHWH-Rohi cause us to embrace God's hedge of protection that is around us and God's Hand of protection that is upon us. We can know that God is not going to let anything happen to us. We can know that God is not going

#Don'tNecessarilySaveTheBestForLast

to let anything get to us because He is YHWH-Nissi, our Banner, and because He is YHWH-Rohi, our Shepherd.

This is why I believe the order does matter, and this is why I teach and promote that we take the Names in the order that I teach them.

Now let me say this: I do not, by any stretch of the imagination, want to suggest that if we take the Names out of the order that I teach them, we have sinned a horrible sin. And I do not want to suggest that it will not work because we did not go in that order. And I am not going to suggest that it messes up the whole program and that your prayer is not going to be answered because you did not start with Elohiym and go from there to El Shaddai and from there to YHWH.

I am not saying anything like that because there are incidences and occurrences and situations and circumstances where the exigency of the matter requires you to get right to the point.

Thus, it is the exigency of the situation that will often determine the order in which you pray the Names. And sometimes, you may not even get to any particular order because the exigency of the matter determines which Name is best for the situation. This is what is meant by the subtitle, "You Can't Necessarily Save the Best for Last." Because what is the best? The best becomes the one that speaks to the crisis, and when faced with a crisis, you need to bring the best up to the front of the line.

When I teach effective prayer and prayer that hits the target, one of the things that I emphasize is that effective prayer needs to be targeted. If the prayer need is healing, and the prayer request is healing, and the news comes from the doctor that Ms. Z has thirty minutes to live, then the best is YHWH-Rapha, the Lord our Healer.

In a case like that, we are not going to have time to go through the list of Names and take ten minutes to talk about

Elohiym and how God created the heavens and the earth or spend fifteen minutes thanking God that He is YHWH-Shammah, the God Who is here with me while at the same time, in Australia with our brothers and sisters there.

In instances such as that, the exigency of the matter dictates what we pray and the order we pray, and we need to identify what is best, by the circumstances, and bring the best to the front of the line. In exigent circumstances, we don't necessarily want to save the best for last. This person has been given thirty minutes to live, so we will need to dispense with the list and dispense with the order, and bombard heaven on behalf of that person, binding the devil and thanking God that He is YHWH-Rapha, the Lord her Healer. In that case, YHWH-Rapha is the best for the situation at hand, so we would not necessarily want to save the best for last.

In the Bible, there was a woman who had an emergency. The Scriptures said she made her way to Jesus and all she had time to say, was "Lord, help me!"

She did not have time to go through: "You are Elohiym, the God Who created all things. We give You praise, O Holy Father, that You created everything with Words and that You changed everything Words. And we thank You, Lord, that You created us in Your image and after Your likeness; and so we bless You today that You are Elohiym; and we thank You today, O God, that You are El Shaddai…"

She did not have time for that. There was an emergency. There was a crisis. She needed God's help. She said, "Lord, help me."

So, I absolutely recognize, understand, and agree that the exigency will dictate the order.

If there is a crisis, the exigency will dictate the order. If we get a word that somebody just got rushed to the hospital, is on his deathbed, was severely injured, and we don't know

#Don'tNecessarilySaveTheBestForLast

if that person is going to make it, we can't go through all of these Names. We need to go right to "Lord, deliver him; Lord, heal him; Lord, move on his behalf. You are YHWH-Rapha. You promised in Your Word. You were wounded for his transgressions. You were bruised for his iniquities." We need to get right there.

Nevertheless, while I insist that we have to yield the order to any crisis or emergency and recognize that the exigency will dictate the order, I am still promoting from the rooftops that when there is no crisis, we should take the Names in order.

And I want to make this clear: because remember, the Bible tells us that the people of God "*always* ought to pray and not lose heart" (Luke 18:1, modified). We *always* ought to be praying, and if we are *always* praying, it is not *always* an emergency. It is not *always* a crisis. Let's not wait for the emergencies and the crises and the exigencies to talk to God.

We should be getting up in the morning talking to God.

We can talk to God while we're taking our shower.

We can talk to God while we're driving to work.

We can talk to God while we're on our break.

We can talk to God on our way back home.

Some people only talk to God for five minutes when it's time to go to bed. No. No. No. He deserves more than that. He deserves better than that.

With what measure you mete it shall be measured to you. We need to spend some time with Him.

So yes, there are times that the exigency dictates the order. But when there is no emergency and the circumstances are not exigent, I strongly recommend that we take the Names in the order taught here because it builds us up and puts us in the position that by the time we get to the real need, our faith is intact, and we are locked in.

DR. MELVIN G. BARNEY, ESQ.

So Who is YHWH? YHWH is too expansive to be able to focus on.

Who is YHWH? YHWH is too immense to be able to contain. The best way to put it is that YHWH is "The I Am That I Am." YHWH is whoever you need Him to be.

Therefore, when the devil tries to tell you that you do not deserve a relationship with God, you can say, "No, no, devil, for He is YHWH-T'Sidkenu, and He has created a relationship with me."

And when the devil tries to make you worry about what might happen down the road, you can say, "Not today, devil, for He is YHWH-Shalom, and I am going to rest in and wait patiently on Him."

And when the devil tries to make you feel like you are never going to get your miracle, you can say, "Get behind me, Satan, for healing is the children's bread, and I am a child of God."

Jesus said, "After this manner pray, say, 'Hallowed be Your Name.'" If we want the manifestation of what the Name entails, we've got to hallow the Name. If we want the manifestation of what the Name promises, we have to hallow the Name. When we hallow the Name, we sow the Name. And the way we sow the Name is to speak the Name.

So we thank You, oh God, that You are YHWH-T'Sidkenu and YHWH-M'Kaddesh. You are our righteousness and the Lord Who sanctifies us. We bless You for the security we have in You, for we know who we are in Christ.

And we praise You, Lord, that You are YHWH-Shalom and YHWH-Shammah. Thank You for perfect peace and for teaching us to be God-inside-minded.

And then we give You praise, O God, that You are YHWH-Rapha and YHWH-Yireh. You are our Healer, and You are our Provider. Thank You for how You heal us from the crown of our heads to the souls of our feet and for how You meet all of our needs, according to Your riches in glory.

And then Lord, we honor You as YHWH-Nissi and YHWH-Rohi, for You are our Banner, the God Who fights for us, and our Shepherd, the One Who takes care of us.

Lord, we thank You for this relationship with You. Thank You that we have the opportunity to get to know You. Thank You for giving us access to You. And thank You for not allowing us to take Your Name in vain. You are teaching us to engage Your Name in our affairs, use it as a tool, sow it as a seed, and utilize it to cause Your will and promises to come to pass in our lives.

There is no God like You. And for Who You are, we celebrate You, we love You, and we give you praise. In Jesus's Name. Hallelujah. Amen.

SCRIPTURE REFERENCES

FOUNDATION SCRIPTURES

Exodus 20:7
Luke 11:2

FREQUENTLY CITED SCRIPTURES

Genesis 1:11-12
Mark 4:13-14
Mark 4:26-29
Luke 8:11

OTHER SCRIPTURAL REFERENCES

Genesis 1:1
Genesis 1:1-3, 11, 26-27, modified
Genesis 2:16-17
Genesis 2:19
Genesis 6:5-7
Genesis 15:1-3
Genesis 15:4-5
Genesis 15:6
Genesis 15:6, KJV
Genesis 15:6, NASB
Genesis 17:1-2

Genesis 18:14
Genesis 22:2
Genesis 22:9-14, modified
Exodus 3:4-6
Exodus 3:13-15, modified
Exodus 5:2
Exodus 6:2-3, modified
Exodus 15:26, modified
Exodus 17:9-16
Exodus 17:14-16, modified
Exodus 20:1-17
Exodus 25:8, 21-22
Exodus 32:21-24
Leviticus 20:7-8
Deuteronomy 8:18
Deuteronomy 28:15, 23, 34, 65-67
Joshua 1:8
Judges 6:23-24
1 Kings 17:10-12
2 Chronicles 20:14-17
2 Chronicles 20:20-21
Psalm 23:1-6
Psalm 51:5
Psalm 63:3-4
Psalm 82:6
Psalm 91:1-2, 5-6, 11-12
Psalm 100:3
Psalm 103:2-3
Psalm 107:20
Proverbs 3:9-10
Proverbs 4:20-22
Proverbs 18:10
Isaiah 1:19

Isaiah 53:4-5
Isaiah 59:19
Isaiah 64:6
Jeremiah 23:6
Lamentations 3:22, KJV
Ezekiel 48:35
Daniel 11:32
Malachi 3:10
Matthew 5:19-20
Matthew 6:25-33
Matthew 8:16-17
Mark 4:3, 8, 13-14
Mark 4:24
Mark 4:24, KJV
Luke 10:17-19
Luke 18:1, modified
John 1:1-3, 14
John 10:1-5
John 10:34
John 14:13-14
John 15:5-7
John 15:16
John 21:15-17
Acts 3:1-8, 11-12, 16
Romans 3:10
Romans 4:22, KJV
Romans 5:1
Romans 8:1-2
Romans 8:31
Romans 8:37
Romans 10:9
Romans 12:18
1 Corinthians 6:19-20

1 Corinthians 12:31
1 Corinthians 15:57
2 Corinthians 5:21
2 Corinthians 6:14-16
2 Corinthians 10:3-5
Galatians 3:13-14
Galatians 6:7
Ephesians 6:10-12
Philippians 2:13
Philippians 4:6-7
Colossians 1:13, modified
Colossians 1:27
Hebrews 11:3
Hebrews 12:14
James 1:6-8
1 Peter 2:9
1 Peter 2:9, KJV
1 Peter 2:24
2 Peter 1:4
1 John 4:4, KJV
3 John 2, KJV

NOTES

Chapter 1

"Don't Leave Home Without It," registered trademark 1975, American Express Company.

The Ten Commandments, copyright 1956, Paramount Pictures Corporation.

Chapter 3

"Stop in the Name of Love," copyright 1965, Brian Holland, Lamont Dozier, Eddie Holland.

"Baby Love," copyright 1964, Brian Holland, Lamont Dozier, Eddie Holland.

"You Keep Me Hanging On," copyright 1966, Brian Holland, Lamont Dozier, Eddie Holland.

"Say My Name!" copyright 1999, Sony Music Entertainment, Inc.

Chapter 7

The Beverly Hillbillies, copyright 1962, CBS Broadcasting Inc.

Chapter 10

Trading Places, copyright 1983, Paramount Pictures Corporation.

Chapter 12

Jerry Maguire, copyright 1996, TriStar Pictures, Inc.

Chapter 14

"Free Your Mind," copyright 1992, En Vogue, copyright Two Tuff-E-Nuff Songs.

Chapter 17

"About Sheep," Compassion in World Farming, accessed April 10, 2021, www.ciwf.com/farmed-animals/sheep.

Sheep 101, accessed April 10, 2021, www.sheep101.info.

ABOUT THE AUTHOR

Dr. Melvin G. Barney, Esq. is the founding pastor of the O Logos Alive Church, of Sacramento California, which was started in 2019, just one year before the pandemic hit, and put us all on a "time-out."

Dr. Barney holds a doctorate in ministry from United Theological Seminary, a juris doctorate from the University of California School of Law, and an MS in Industrial Administration (MBA) from the Carnegie Mellon University Graduate School of Industrial Administration. As an attorney, he started his legal career with the Law Office of Johnnie L. Cochran, Jr., worked on the O. J. Simpson's "Trial of the Century," and had the opportunity to become involved with other high-profile clients, including Michael Jackson and George Clinton.

As a minister of the gospel, Melvin brings to the table a distinguished yet unique set of business, legal, and ministerial credentials that enables him to balance the business with the spiritual and to reach and relate to white-collars and blue-collars alike. Some have analogized his preaching style to that of a lawyer whose objective is to "prove his case for the Lord."

Dr. Barney has a unique ability to teach the Word in such a way that makes it come alive and causes people to want to grow closer to God. From the "Soteria Seminar," which is designed to equip the child of God with foundational teachings and solutions from the Word of God about our great salvation, to the "Eight Weeks of Healing," which provides a prescription for resuscitating, healing, and reviving a church and a people who have been through trauma, to the Koinonia Teachings, which coach the hearers to aspire to a higher level of intimacy in their relationships with God and with one another, Dr. Barney challenges God's people to embrace the promises of God, to pursue an intimate relationship with the Lord, and to walk in the unity that makes God's people invincible.

CPSIA information can be obtained
at www.ICGtesting.com
Printed in the USA
JSHW021919290722
28684JS00001B/1